FROM
BROKEN TO
Brave

Profound life & business lessons
learned on my journey through pain, loss and
abuse to successful *entrepreneur*

Dear Joy,

Thank you very much for your
support; I hope you enjoy the
rest of the story.

Sam Pea

xxx

S A M   P E A R C E

Cover image by: Rudi Design, 99Designs
Book design by: SWATT Books Ltd

Printed in the United Kingdom
First Printing, 2020

ISBN: 978-1-9160776-4-5 (Paperback)
ISBN: 978-1-9160776-5-2 (eBook)

SWATT Books Ltd.
Southampton, SO19 7QN

www.swatt-books.co.uk

This book is dedicated to those who dared to say, 'Enough is enough'.

Acknowledgements

One thing I have learned on this journey, and the journeys I help take my clients through, is that a great author is much like a great king – a large proportion of that greatness comes from behind the throne. There are many people who, directly or indirectly, helped make this book possible who I would like to thank.

First and foremost, I want to thank my parents and in particular my mum Marion. I know this process was just as painful for you as it was for me – maybe even more so. But your understanding, patience and encouragement helped me through it so that I can finally put my demons to bed.

My loving husband Nathan. You stood by me through all the pain and chaos. You've been my rock in the storm and my guiding light through the darkest night. I will never be able to express how much I rely on your love and support. You give me strength, and together we can conquer the world.

My best friends Greg and Paul. Greg: you are my only connection to a world long lost but never forgotten. Thank you for reminding me who I once was, and for your constant encouragement. Paul: you were the first to know about this project and many of the stories contained within it. Your belief in both me and this project has been invaluable; I just hope that I can soon return the favour.

My business mentors, Ian Dickson and Brad Burton. Though you were each unaware of it at the time, you both provided me with the tools to be able to put the pieces of my life back together and give me purpose.

My editor Mark Beaumont-Thomas. Thank you for helping me dig that little bit deeper to bring my story to life. My achievement with the Page Turner Awards is thanks in no small part to your sterling dedication and hard work.

Finally, I want to thank all the unnamed faces that have touched my life at some time or another. Without you, and the experiences I had as a result of you being a part of my journey, I would not be the person I am today.

Table of Contents

Introduction

It's no secret to anyone who knows me that I am a profoundly private person. I don't believe in airing my personal life for the world to see. It's the reason why I'm not very active on social media outside of my business, and why I'm rarely the life and soul of the party (unless I have to be).

I guess that is common for a lot of people; however, I can sometimes take that to extremes. There are of course a few people close to me that know certain things about my past and my life, but no one – not even my parents or my husband – know the full story. Not one person other than myself is aware of all the pieces and how they have fitted together over the years to make me the person I am today.

Looking back on my life I don't really know if that was ever an intentional choice or if that's just the way I developed.

Whether it was a defence mechanism or just an in-built personality trait; like how some people are naturally outgoing or charismatic. But things started to change in my mind regarding that point not all that long ago.

Whilst writing my first book, *Stress-Free Self-Publishing*, which was published in May 2019, a couple of my beta readers, as well as a good friend who is a book writing mentor, pointed out that there was nothing about me in the book apart from the very sparse author bio I had reluctantly added to the back matter. Even that I had just taken from my website and padded out slightly. When I asked why that mattered when the book was meant as a how-to guide, everyone's response was similar... it helps readers to get to know more about you and connect with you as a real person. The more human you appear as an author, the more they will engage with the content of your book.

Being the rather stubborn and headstrong person that I am, I didn't relent very much in regards to adding anything personal to *Stress-Free Self-Publishing*. However, it did plant the seed of starting to see how other people might find value in my experiences... if I would just be willing to open up and share them. The more I thought about the idea, the more it grew on me. I had always wanted to help people in any way I could, and here was a way that I could help others that I had never considered before – by sharing some of my experiences in the hope that someone else could learn from my mistakes.

I decided to put this theory to the test by presenting a 4Sight to one of my local 4Networking groups. 4Sights are an opportunity to give a brief presentation on any chosen topic (as long as it's not a sales pitch) at my business networking group of choice, 4Networking. The 20-minute talk touched on a few memories and lessons that eventually formed Chapters 4, 9 and 10 of this book.

It was the most difficult talk I have ever given! This was the first time I had spoken about these experiences out loud, and I was doing it to a roomful of fellow business owners who I only saw maybe once a month, if ever. I had one or two friends in the room who I had asked to come along for support, but for the most part I barely knew anyone in the audience of 20 all that well.

As I started to speak, I kept thinking to myself: "How are these people going to react? What will they think of me after this? Will they think less of me? Am I going to ruin the professional reputation that I have worked to build with these people?" Despite my thoughts running a mile a minute and my emotions in turmoil over digging up past memories, I made it to the end of the talk. There was a stunned silence followed by genuine, heartfelt applause; and I had to choke back tears of relief.

I went on to explain that what I had just shared was going to form part of a new book that I was writing, intended to help people cope with similar experiences, and asked if they found any value in what I had just shared. The answer was a resounding yes. So not five days after *Stress-Free*

Self-Publishing hit the shelves, I started writing the initial manuscript for *From Broken to Brave*.

***

Despite this rather secretive preamble, my life has not been particularly extraordinary. At the tender age of 42, I can appreciate that it's not been that long either. I'm also acutely aware that there are people in this world who have had a far worse time in life than I have, but I have had more than my fair share of tough times and bad experiences. My family moved around a lot when I was a kid which meant that I found it very difficult to make new friends (despite the practice) and as a result I was bullied mercilessly all the way through school. As you will soon read, particular circumstances led me to become addicted to drugs and on the edge of suicide. I have been completely broke, relying on food banks and begging for my next meal.

But this book is not a "woe is me" story. No. With the benefit of hindsight, I've been able to glean the powerful and profound lessons that these and many other experiences have taught me about life as well as running a business. Some have been more obvious than others; some have taken me decades to learn and even longer to live by. But they are the lessons that have shaped who I am and the way I view the world.

I want to share some of these experiences with you in the hope that the lessons I have learned will somehow help you. My wish is that, by drawing back the curtain on my life and sharing some of my story, you may find answers to questions that you are facing in your own life. Or perhaps you will find the strength and resolve to cope with similar situations that I have overcome. Maybe you will simply find solace in knowing that you're not alone; that someone has walked in your shoes before you and not only survived but thrived.

Though many of the experiences and stories that I am about to share with you are very dark, I have written this book as a beacon of hope to show that no obstacle is permanent, no heartbreak unrecoverable, and nothing is ever broken forever. In these pages you will learn of some of the pain, loss, fear, setbacks, and what at the time felt like insurmountable odds, that I have faced to get to where I am right now; but also come to know that despite all that has happened in my life (or maybe because of it) I am the woman I am today. Confident, strong and successful, whilst also remaining caring, gentle and committed to helping better both myself and the world around me.

Life is an opportunity,
benefit from it.
Life is beauty, admire it.
Life is a dream, realise it.
Life is a challenge, meet it.
Life is a duty, complete it.
Life is a game, play it.
Life is a promise, fulfil it.
Life is sorrow, overcome it.

Life is a song, sing it.

Life is a struggle, accept it.

Life is a tragedy, confront it.

Life is an adventure, dare it.

Life is luck, make it.

Life is too precious,

do not destroy it.

Life is life, fight for it.

– Mother Teresa; Roman Catholic nun,
missionary and humanitarian

ONE:

Gravy fries are not the answer

Despite popular opinion, even among those who know me, I was born in the UK and not in Canada. My dad is British and in his youth was a radar technician in the Royal Air Force. He met my mother when he was stationed in Goose Bay, Labrador on cold weather training with Tornado Squadron. My mum was a teacher at a nearby school where all the base personnel sent their kids while stationed there. According to the story, they met in the Bulldog Club one evening when Dad was on leave and she proceeded to drink him under the table. It was love at first sight... once he was sober again that is. Dad maintains to this day that the bartender was serving him doubles and my mum singles in the hopes of "lending him a hand"; but it's hilarious either way.

As always happens in the military, Dad's posting eventually came to an end and he was shipped back to the UK. After a year of missing him terribly, Mum decided that he was the one and upended her life to move to the UK. Shortly after, they were married, and I came along in late January 1978.

Reflecting now on Mum's dramatic decision to leave behind everything she knew in pursuit of love and how much it correlates with dramatic and life-altering decisions that I have taken in my own life, I suppose it's little wonder that my story takes some of the twists and turns that it does. But I digress.

Mum had always wanted me to have a Canadian education. I've never really discussed it at length with her as to why she felt that way, but seeing as I was only 5 years old at the time that our little family relocated from Camberley in Surrey to a quiet suburb outside Toronto, Canada, I didn't have much say in the matter.

I don't really remember very much about my early years in school; either in the UK or once we moved to Canada. I have fleeting memories of what my junior school classroom looked like: the layout of the playground and the route I used to walk to school. My main memories of that period of my life seem to pick up when I transferred from junior school to The Valleys senior school.

The school was located in the same grounds as The Valleys recreation centre, which housed an indoor ice rink, a basketball court and a couple of public studio spaces. During lunch breaks, all the 'cool kids' used to congregate in the lobby of the rec. centre where there was a little café that served the best gravy fries I've ever had. Funnily enough, I've gone off gravy fries permanently and I sometimes wonder if that has anything to do with this particular incident.

I don't remember being bullied at either of the two other schools I attended when I first moved to Canada, but for some reason The Valleys was different. It seemed that nothing I did was deemed 'right' by the other kids. My English accent, which wasn't very thick but was still quite noticeable, was always an easy target for kids to make fun of. My family was never hard up for money, but we weren't well-off either, so my parents couldn't afford the latest trainers or brand-name clothes that were the requirement for being accepted by the in-crowd. But worst of all was the fact that I went through puberty quite early; much earlier than nearly all of my classmates, and certainly faster than my education on the subject could keep up with. This resulted in a number of embarrassing incidents with premature periods and body odour issues, which in turn led to relentless bullying by nearly all the other kids, 'cool' or not.

As a result, I only had one friend that I can remember from that school: another outcast called Jennifer. She was targeted for abuse simply because of her looks. She was very gangly, always quite clumsy, and had very prominent buck teeth. Jennifer and I naturally hung out together, simply because no one else would.

One day, late in my first year at The Valleys, I remember walking into the rec. centre to buy some fries from the café for lunch when I heard a group of kids pestering Jennifer relentlessly for her lunch money. I don't remember what lame excuses they were using as their reasoning for needing HER lunch money instead of using their own, but they were starting to get quite aggressive about the whole thing.

I have never been one to step into the middle of an argument, especially one that was looking like it would deteriorate into a fight, but I have always been extremely loyal to my friends. Without a second thought, I waded into the argument and offered my lunch money if they would leave Jennifer alone. THAT turned out to be a monumental mistake!

Jennifer immediately turned on me, saying that she could take care of herself and didn't need anyone to rescue her, and then stormed off. I was quite shocked and suddenly very confused... I was trying to help, and the person I thought I was helping was mad at me for it!

It took several weeks of trying to explain my motivations and why I did what I did in order to convince Jennifer to start speaking to me again. When she eventually did forgive me, she explained that by doing what I had done, it made her appear even weaker than she had before the incident. The bullies now had more ammunition in their arsenal, with the extra dig that she needed me to protect her. This was something that hadn't dawned on me at the time. It was true though. I had heard the new taunts several times, which only intensified when I entered the room.

My rash act that day also made my own situation with the bullies worse. I was now the daily target for the extortion of lunch money. Not a day went by that I wasn't harassed by at least one person to buy them lunch or give them money for the bus. At first, I thought that it meant I was slowly being accepted by the other kids and that this was my way into the 'in-crowd'.

One day when Mum asked why I was always now so hungry when I got home from school, I told her I was giving away my lunch money. She gave me that look that she always did when she thought I should know better. I tried to justify my actions by explaining that I was helping friends in need, but she soon divested me of that notion. She made me realise that they were just taking advantage of my generosity and weren't actually interested in being friends with me.

I felt so stupid... and gullible. I tried to turn the tide, but by that time the precedent had been set and it was extremely difficult to stand my ground by refusing to hand over my meagre lunch money every day. It took time... a long time, as well as the odd bump and bruise when things got a bit physical, but eventually the bullies started to leave me alone for more tractable prey.

I have tried my best to not let that incident all those years ago make me jaded towards people who ask for money, but it has given me a zero-tolerance attitude towards those who take advantage of the weak; whether it be physical, financial, or any other form of dominance. It's just a shame that this attitude has never seemed to extend to people taking advantage of me. To this day that is still a bit of a blind spot in my character, but we'll touch on that a bit later.

"Sometimes it is better to lose and do the right thing, than win and do the wrong thing."

– Tony Blair; former British prime minister

Lesson Learned

The lesson I learned from that one act of trying to help a friend but making things a million times worse, is a bit of an ambiguous one. On the one hand it is an honourable and noble thing to want to do the right thing and help those in need, but every now and then what you deem as the "right thing" may not be the best thing in that situation.

If you're anything like me, you are often led by your heart in situations like this one. Emotion, whether it be loyalty, protection, sympathy or pity, can lead you to make rash decisions in the moment, without thinking things through. We believe so deeply in our heart that our action is warranted that we rarely look at the bigger picture – we simply act.

There are some people that will read this and think that point of view is a little too clinical, and possibly think that I am suggesting not to help others in need; and that is NOT what I am suggesting at all. I simply suggest that you look at the WAY in which you are trying to help and take a second to think if it is the BEST way to help.

There is an old proverb that states: give a man a fish and he eats for a day; teach a man how to fish and you feed him for a lifetime. Think about whether what you are doing to help is just a temporary band-aid to a wider problem, or whether it will be more harmful in the long run. If it is (or at least has the potential to be), I suggest you re-evaluate how you want to help.

There is a second lesson here that I didn't learn until much later in my life, that also reflects on this situation, and that is to pick your battles. Not every fight is worth the effort of fighting. If the gain from winning a battle isn't worth the effort, pain, aggravation, scars or heartache, then it's a fight best left for another day or to be fought in a different way.

In the situation with Jennifer, were the months of increased bullying of both myself and Jennifer worth the 24 hours of respite that my actions gave her that day? Of course not. Is the fight against bullying in general worth fighting? Of course it is. And this is why it is important to pause for a second BEFORE you simply act.

Are your actions going to cause more harm than good? Are you simply postponing the inevitable? Are you acting for your benefit or theirs? These questions only need take a second to think about but will result in you truly being able to help a situation.

"All beings tremble before violence. All fear death. All love life. See yourself in others. Then whom can you hurt? What harm can you do?"

– Buddha

TWO:

Shock tactics

Things started to change somewhat when I moved on to high school. My family had moved house (again) which meant that I ended up in a different school catchment area than most of the kids I went to The Valleys with, so it gave me the chance for a fresh start.

I still wasn't one of the 'cool' kids, but I did find my way into the small clique of 'grunge' kids. The grunge scene was in full swing in the early '90s, influenced by the music of Nirvana, Pearl Jam and Soundgarden. The scruffy clothing style that went with Seattle grunge music suited me, and my budget, down to the ground. Aside from needing to save up for a whole summer to buy a pair of 9-hole Doc Martens, I could find most quintessential grunge clothes (frayed jeans, old band t-shirts and plaid flannel shirts) at flea markets and charity shops.

I finally felt part of a group, and accepted, albeit by a very small minority. We would all sit together playing cards at lunch in the cafeteria or in the back of the library whenever we had a free period. There was still a small aspect of bullying, but we were targeted as a group as opposed to any one individual. The strength in numbers made it a bit easier to deal with.

Outside of my close-knit group of friends, I was still very quiet and withdrawn. I tried to do my best in class, but outside of answering teachers' questions I didn't talk very much and kept to myself until I was back in the relative safety of my group of friends. This meant that most people just didn't notice me at all, which at the time suited me just fine. I didn't want to be the centre of attention, because attention usually meant being the butt of some joke or being picked on for some obscure teenage social faux pas. The one exception to that was when I was in music class.

I majored in music throughout high school, playing both flute and piano, and had plans of joining the Toronto Symphony Orchestra (TSO) on graduation. I had at least one music class every semester; I was the lead flautist in the school band and took private piano lessons where I excelled to Royal Conservatory level 12. I even tried to learn to play the guitar, but found that the cuts and raw fingers I got from practising interfered with being able to play the flute and the piano to the level that I was accustomed to, so I gave it up.

I loved music; no matter the style or genre, I found deeper meaning to all the things I experienced through music. And not just playing it but listening to it as well. This was the time that Napster hit the internet and I was hooked; spending hours exploring new music and finding connections between bands and artists. I thought I had found my calling in life and was convinced that I had it all figured out. Then a series of three outwardly unrelated events happened during my senior year that changed everything.

The first was the audition. Not just any audition, but *THE* audition that if I passed would see me transfer from my current high school to the one school in the area that had a dedicated music program that would all but guarantee me a place on the roster for the Royal College of Music and put me on the fast track to join the TSO.

I practised for weeks, 4-5 hours a day leading up to that audition. My parents paid for extra tuition to make sure that my technique was as perfect as I could muster. I studied all the music theory I could get my hands on and brushed up on as much history as I could so that I was prepared for any question the panel of judges could throw at me. When audition day finally rolled around, I was convinced that I was ready.

The reality was that I wasn't ready, not by a long shot. The other kids in that audition had been playing their instruments of choice all their lives, whereas I had only learned both the piano and the flute four years prior. The judges commended me on how much I had learned in that short period of time, and that they would be interested to see me again once I had a few more years of experience and practice, but for now I didn't have what it would take.

I was devastated. To be told that the countless hours of practice, studying and extra tuition wasn't enough, that after all that I still wasn't good enough, broke my heart. In a sense it also broke my love of music. I pretty much stopped playing after that. I was now at a complete loss as to what my future would hold for me. I had so pinned all my hopes and dreams on that one audition that I had no contingency plan for what I would do if it didn't work out.

This led to event number two, the apprenticeship.

My high school was a part of an apprenticeship initiative being trialed in Ontario at the time. An experimental programme intended to give students experience of the world of work before they went onto college or university, in the hope of producing a more dedicated and driven workforce. The idea being to help teenagers not only to decide what they wanted to do once they left school but to give them some experience of doing that job to be sure they had made the right choice *before* spending 4+ years in post-secondary education and racking up the thousands of dollars of debt that went with it.

Up until that point I knew what type of apprenticeship I had wanted to do in my final semester, but now I had no idea. I had hinged everything on that one audition, that would lead me down one career path, and I had been told I didn't have what it takes. My guidance counsellor at the time understood my situation and suggested that I take a psychometric test to figure out what else I might be good at.

The test consisted of dozens of the most random questions I had ever seen; completely unrelated to each other or anything that I would have attributed to a specific line of work or skill set. But apparently the results of the test indicated a strong inclination for computer sciences and art, so the counsellor put me forward for an apprenticeship at a graphic design studio.

At the time, I found the entire process to be completely ridiculous, but seeing as I didn't have any other ideas of what I wanted to do with my life, I went along with it. I did know my way around computers. Dad, after leaving the military, had become a computer storage engineer and had bought me my first computer when I was just 3, so I had literally grown up with the things. As for the art, I just couldn't see it. Sure, I liked looking at art; I remember being fascinated by the artwork on Dad's vinyl collection growing up, but I couldn't draw to save my life, so didn't see how this was going to work out at all.

How wrong was I?! I loved my apprenticeship almost from day one. My lack of skills in fine art didn't make any difference, as the computer did most of the work. It just needed a vision of what would and wouldn't work, which I did have. I picked up the necessary skills very quickly, and before my 8-week apprenticeship was finished, my first piece of design work had been approved and printed. Seeing my work out in the world for everyone to look at and judge was unlike anything I had experienced before. All thoughts of joining the TSO were gone and I was now laser-focused on what I needed to become a graphic designer.

It turned out that I needed quite a bit more than a 2-month apprenticeship in order to qualify for a place at a design college, but I was determined to do whatever was necessary to get that place. With the help of my guidance counsellor, I managed to secure a provisional acceptance at George Brown College of Art & Design in Toronto on the condition that I took – and passed – the pre-requisite art classes before I could enrol. So, while all my friends graduated that year, I stayed behind for an extra semester to take the required classes.

That additional semester led to random event number three, the club.

High school had not only introduced me to friends, it had also introduced me to the idea of boyfriends. One of my boyfriends had introduced me to a group of his friends that didn't go to our school. Some had left high school already, others lived slightly further away. I never did get to the bottom of how this specific group had originally formed.

There was one member of that little group that I got on really well with, and that was Mike. Mike had been an outcast his entire life, just like me, but seemed to embrace that far more comfortably than I did. He and I had similar tastes in literature, and he had introduced me to authors like David Eddings and James Redfield.

I don't really remember how the conversation came up, but Mike invited me to go with him to a nightclub that he frequented downtown that he thought I might really like. He described it as a haven for outcasts and people who didn't fit into any conventional stereotype. I was intrigued and so went along to see what it was all about. And that was my introduction to The Sanctuary Vampire Sex Bar, the oldest goth club in north America.

I was enthralled the moment I walked through the doors. It was dark, dingy, smoky, and none too clean, but that wasn't what fascinated me. It was the combination of theatrics and blatant disregard for what society deemed as 'normal' that seemed to emanate from every person there that spoke volumes to me. Here was a group of people completely free to be themselves in whatever form that took, with no fear of judgment or ridicule. Mike explained to me that this was the one place he felt truly safe to be himself, and that this was a culture that protected its own. I could feel it calling to me, that maybe I had finally found my 'sanctuary' too.

Before long, I was a regular visitor to Sanctuary and the more I learned about the underground goth culture surrounding the club, the more it fascinated me. By this time, I had finished the additional semester that I needed to take to accumulate the credits required to take my place at George Brown. So, I pretty much had 9 months off school between finishing my last class at TL Kennedy High School in January, to starting my first year of college in September. That period was spent working to save up for my tuition and going to the club every chance I got.

Needless to say, those 9 months had a profound effect on me; not only on my outlook on life but my whole perception of who I was and how I portrayed myself to the world. Outwardly I started wearing all black, cut my hair really short and died it black with red streaks in the front. You should see the pictures! But the biggest change was in my demeanour and attitude. The freedom of not feeling that I needed to conform to be accepted meant that my confidence started to increase dramatically. I started to relax into my own skin more and found the courage to start dancing at the club, which in itself gave me an outlet for my passion for music that I had not explored before. My dancing brought me out of the shadows and into the centre of attention, and surprisingly I found that I really liked it, which just fuelled my confidence even more.

Most people associate goth culture as just a bunch of angst-ridden teenagers swanning around all in black writing bad poetry as a rebellion against mommy and daddy. Now, don't get me wrong, there are a fair number of goths for whom that is the full extent of their involvement. But for me, the more I learned about the underlying motivations behind goth culture, the more it resonated with me. To me, being a goth was more of a social commentary against mainstream media and society as a whole dictating what was acceptable as 'normal' than any outright rebellion. It was the freedom to express your true self in whatever way felt right to you – through clothing, dance, art, literature or style. And I embraced it mind, body and soul.

By the time that my high school graduation ceremony came around in August 1997, my transformation was complete. Unless you had known me really well, you wouldn't have recognised the person who walked into the auditorium that night. Jet black pixie short hair, a floor-length Morticia-style black velvet dress and stiletto heels, cloaked in an air of quiet confidence that dared anyone to challenge my choice of appearance – I was like something out of a Bela Lugosi film.

The majority of my classmates had graduated the year before, but there were a few people there that I knew; either class mates from the art classes that I had remained behind to take or those with younger brothers or sisters who were graduating with the class that year. Aside from the few people who I made a point to go and speak to, I remained somewhat to myself at the back of the auditorium. This was not out of any shyness or insecurity, but more a reflection on just how much I had changed since I had last been in that building, and quietly amusing myself with the notion that hardly anyone recognised me.

Having a last name of Watt (my maiden name) meant that I had to wait until near the end of the evening before being called up to receive my diploma, but I remember that moment vividly. On hearing my name, I confidently walked down the centre isle of the auditorium to the stage. I could hear people whispering as I walked past, "Oh my God, is that Samantha? She looks so different!" Hearing those whispers ripple through the auditorium gave me a warm feeling of satisfaction. I might have been a wallflower while I had been there, but I was certainly leaving high school with a bang!

"Change is painful, but nothing is as painful as staying stuck somewhere you don't belong"

Mandy Hale; New York Times bestselling author

Lesson Learned

The lesson that I learned from that summer of transformation and redefining myself was that radical change is always easier to achieve when no one is looking.

Scrutiny of any kind always has a tendency to make us second-guess ourselves. We worry whether the change that we are wanting to make is the right one, and whether it will be well received by those we care about or by society in general. This second guessing can lead to indecision, or worse still, making decisions based on the wrong motivations.

If you are considering a dramatic change of any kind, whether it be in your job, your appearance, your relationships, even your view on the world, you need space to explore the idea of that change in isolation first. You need to be able to work out the parameters of that change in how it relates to you before you can realistically evaluate how it relates to others.

If I had attempted to redefine myself as I did while I was still attending high school, I would have faced daily questions and potential ridicule for doing something different than what everyone associated with me. As a result, I would have questioned whether the change was worth the aggravation and would probably have bowed to peer pressure and not gone through with it to the extent that I did.

But that summer, separated from my previous peer group, meant I had the space to explore the change that I was going through and find how it felt the most comfortable for me. So that when I did present the 'new me' to my old peers and classmates, I was confident in my decision and could own the change that I had made.

I'm not suggesting that you need to take yourself completely out of your situation for six months in order to make a big change in your life, but you need to give yourself a bit of space to think through your decisions with little or no outside influence – at least until you are comfortable with the idea of your change. That way you will not be as easily swayed by the opinion of others and will be able to rationally weigh that opinion against your own values and reasoning for wanting to change.

Change is a very scary thing. Not only for the person undergoing the change, but also for those around them. Change is usually accompanied by some amount of additional instability. That instability will affect those around you, whether you intend it to or not. But, if you have taken the time and space to evaluate why you are embarking on the change and are confident that this change is the best thing for you in the long run, it allows you to articulate those reasons to those you care about. Your confidence will also reassure those around you that everything will be OK.

In the beginning, my parents weren't entirely thrilled by the whole goth thing. But as they saw my confidence increase, and listened to me describe why goth culture appealed to me so much, they started to come around to the idea. Once they realised there was no harm in what I was doing and that I was safe not only at the club but also in public in general, they even started to embrace it. Mum started to find amusement in watching other people's reaction to me when we were out in public together. If I hadn't taken my time to explore how and why goth culture appealed to me so much, I wouldn't have been able to set my parents' concerns at ease. Their concerns could then have started to influence my judgement.

So yes, change can be scary and disruptive; but it can also be very liberating and open the door to new opportunities and avenues previously unavailable to you. Take the time to explore change so that you can ensure it is the right change for you.

Once you know in your gut that it is right for you, don't let anything stand in your way and have the courage to follow your convictions.

"It takes a lot of courage to release the familiar and seemingly secure, to embrace the new. But there is no real security in what is no longer meaningful. There is more security in the adventurous and exciting, for in movement there is life, and in change there is power."

– Alan Cohen; inspirational author

THREE:

Clash of the egos

My time spent at George Brown College learning the art of graphic design was both enlightening and challenging. Enlightening in that it gave me the freedom to further explore my personal 'brand' in conjunction with how it related to the world around me. I learned to refine my ideas and my very identity through what I was learning about the creative process and apply that learning to not only my work but my very existence. Design and creative interpretation became my universal language for everything that I experienced, and I just couldn't get enough of it.

I started to analyse everything around me that had a design element to it, like magazines, art, cinema and products. On top of that, I started to apply the theories that I was learning about design, such as balance, ratio, and cause and effect, to wider, more abstract concepts like society, personal interaction, and the media.

College was also challenging in the sudden requirement to balance all the trappings of adult life. Class work; a part-time job to pay for the books and art supplies that my student loan didn't cover; maintaining my new-found social life at Sanctuary; all this took some juggling. Couple all of that with the fact that I was still living in Mississauga with my parents, which meant a two-hour commute each way to and from college. Needless to say, having to wake up at 5am in order to make an 8am lecture every day helped me to develop the uncanny ability to be able to sleep on the bus or train and instinctively wake up just before my stop. A necessary life skill for anyone holding down two jobs and going to college full time.

But despite the pressures of suddenly needing to be an adult, I can honestly say that those years were some of the happiest I have had. Life was good. I had loads of friends, both in school and in the club. I had found a place where I felt I belonged, and my confidence blossomed.

I can't remember exactly how it came about, but during my final year at George Brown, I was offered a job at a small design agency specialising in advertising for the travel and tourism industry. Naively I thought this must be my big break. If an agency is wanting to give me a job before I've even graduated it must mean that I'm pretty damn good. I'd be stupid to pass up the opportunity to become a paid graphic designer in order to finish my final semester. So, I dropped out of college, took the job and moved into a flat downtown.

Though I learned a lot in the first few weeks working in the agency, I need to admit (in hindsight) that my cockiness started to get the better of me. My confidence, coupled with a misplaced belief in my abilities stemming from being offered a permanent design job before even graduating, made me uncharacteristically outspoken. As time went on, a personality conflict developed between me and the principal designer (and agency owner) Carol. We had differing opinions on a great many things, from politics and social responsibility to mass media and popular culture. I did my best to keep my opinions to myself when it came to my work and design, though there were a great many aspects where I disagreed with her way of doing things. But when it came to everything else, I just couldn't keep my mouth shut.

Our working relationship became more and more fractious as time went on. We never had any out and out arguments, but I could tell that she just didn't really like me very much. I chalked it up to me not outwardly being what most people would call 'normal' and left it at that. I viewed it as yet another example of mainstream society deeming what was acceptable based on physical appearance and mannerisms as opposed to what I believed mattered most – thought, intellect and ability. It all came to a head one morning when I arrived to work and made a comment regarding what I saw as a correlation between social class and the type of newspaper people read. Going so far as to say that newspapers like the Sun and National Enquirer were written purely for the uneducated. It turned out that Carol read the Sun newspaper on a fairly regular basis and naturally took offence at the comment.

A week or so after that incident I fell seriously ill and spent all day Friday in hospital. During all the commotion, I neglected to call in and let Carol know about the situation. When I did return to work the following Monday, Carol very unceremoniously fired me, having jumped to the conclusion that I had gone out partying instead of coming into work. The huge personality conflict that had grown up between us over the previous months made it impossible for me to argue my case in any way that would make Carol listen, and I left feeling a tempest of conflicting emotions.

My confidence was instantly shattered. I felt confused, scapegoated, ignored, ashamed, angry, and most of all betrayed. All these emotions were then compounded when I learned that I couldn't go back to college to pick up where I had left off as not only had my student loan expired but I would have to take the full year again, as the semester had already finished.

I suddenly found myself very lost and at odds with both myself and where I was going to go from here. The whole experience had a very strange effect on me and the thought of finding another job filled me with irrational panic. The thought that I might not be able to pursue my new-found passion for design if I couldn't resolve this situation led to a deep depression. What further compounded the issue was the simple fact that without a job or a student loan, I had to move back home – the first of several failed attempts to find independence.

I eventually started seeing a therapist to try and work through the emotions that my first experience of working life had generated. I desperately wanted to be a professional designer and contribute in a meaningful way to society, but at the same time I feared how I would be treated by that same society.

It also started to become painfully obvious just how much of a monumental mistake leaving college early had been. That final semester that I didn't think I needed, ended up being the semester that prepared you for life as a working professional designer. And with no means of being able to pay for it, I had to own up to the fact that I would have to pursue my career without that vital preparation.

It took some time and plenty of therapy, but I eventually worked through the emotional baggage that I had picked up during my first real experience of work, and was able to return to a mental state where I could face entering back into employment. My confidence levels did return, but nowhere near the levels that they had been previously, and maybe that was for the best. A healthy dose of humility was sorely needed now that I needed to find a new job as a designer while explaining that I hadn't actually finished my degree.

"Everyone does not have to like you. That is not their job. Liking you is not anyone's purpose in life except yours."

– *Iyanla Vanzant; American inspirational speaker & life coach*

Lesson Learned

The very few people who know that I dropped out of college before being able to obtain my degree always ask me whether I view that as a mistake or not. The truth is that I'm very much on the fence about whether that decision was right or wrong. On the one hand I missed out on a critical part of my preparation for working life as a designer, and I have no doubt that my career would have been much easier, smoother, and possibly more successful, if I had stayed in college. However, I've done pretty well for myself despite dropping out.

I knew I had missed out on vital aspects of my education in terms of career development and preparedness. However, I had gained all of the theory and foundation that I needed, which is very difficult to learn on your own. And it turned out that, as far as the career aspects are concerned, I was able to learn 'on the job' and by continuing my learning wherever I could through books and the internet (despite its fledgling state at the time).

So, looking back with the benefit of 20 years of life experience, yes, dropping out of college was a mistake and one that I would urge any young person NOT to make. But, if circumstances present themselves that put you in the position that you cannot finish a post-secondary education, it's not the end of the world. Many successful people across a wide variety of professions have been able to forge amazing careers for themselves without the benefit of formal extended education. Equally, there are people with diplomas, doctorates and accreditations as long as your arm who only ever lead mediocre lives. It's not your circumstances, but what you make of those circumstances that defines you.

Though that is a profound realisation that I have since come to in later life, that wasn't the main lesson that I learned from that particular experience.

The main lessons that I learned from my first fateful experience of professional working life were two-fold. The first being that not everyone is going to like you, and that's OK. The second being that with confidence comes the need to learn when to speak your mind and when to keep your opinions to yourself.

Human beings are quintessentially pack animals – we naturally live in families, communities and societies, and have an ingrained need to feel accepted by the collective group. Whether we always admit it to ourselves or not, we keenly feel it when a member of the group doesn't like us for whatever reason.

As humanity has evolved, and our societies have become larger and larger, it is less vital to the wellbeing of the society that every member gets along. Which is a good thing, because as a society grows the greater the number of differing personalities it contains, which then in turn means greater potential for conflict.

It's a simple fact that you are not going to like everyone you meet. You may have differing opinions and priorities, different values or you may process information in a different way. It can even be down to factors as superficial as the way a person looks, talks or even moves. There are a thousand and one reasons why two people may not like each other. And that is OK... as long as those two people can still function effectively together within the community.

That's the vital point of difference. You don't have to like someone in order to share space with them – whether that be in a family, job or social group; but you do need to at least be able to get along with them for society to function. This is where the second point of the lesson comes in – learning when to speak your mind and when to keep your mouth shut.

The fact that Carol and I had different opinions on pretty much everything did not mean that we couldn't work effectively together. In fact, we could have had some interesting and healthy intellectual debates to explore our different opinions. Instead, what happened was that I didn't think before expressing some of my opinions and as a result ended up driving a wedge between the two of us that at a critical moment made it impossible for us to come to an understanding.

Increased confidence can often be a double-edged sword. The confidence that makes us believe that our thoughts and opinions do have value can sometimes lead us, if we are not careful, to voicing those thoughts and opinions inappropriately. For someone just finding a new level of confidence, it can be difficult to moderate that confidence and censor your opinion until you ascertain whether that opinion is appropriate in a given situation. Or, at the very least, ascertaining the most appropriate way of voicing your opinion if it is something that you feel needs to be said even if it might cause offence.

Internal censorship can be a difficult lesson to learn; much harder than accepting that not everyone is going to like you. It is one that I still find trips me up every now and then if I'm not careful. I do believe that every opinion has value to the person whose opinion it is, and quite often also to wider society, but not always. So, it is vital to learn the skill of determining when and how to speak your mind to best benefit not only yourself, but society as a whole.

"**Wise men speak because they have something to say; fools because they have to say something.**"

– Plato; Greek philosopher

FOUR:

Hindsight hurts

During my years spent submerged in Toronto's subterranean goth culture at Sanctuary, many guys came into and went out of my life. Most were short-lived, more conquests then actual relationships, often pursued more for the sense of power and control that I felt being in command for the first time in my life than for any true attraction. There were the odd exceptions to the rule, and Mark was the most exceptional of the bunch.

Mark was the resident joker of the club. Everyone knew him, and he had earned the nickname 'Candyman' for several different reasons, not least for the fact that he could be relied upon to source the various drugs of choice for Sanctuary regulars. He was outwardly laid back, funny, appeared never to take anything too seriously, and was training to be a chef. The fact that he was gorgeous as well made him all the more appealing.

We dated for about 6-8 months before our adolescence minds in all their hormone-fuelled wisdom decided that this was 'love' and started talking about more permanent arrangements. It wasn't long afterwards that on the streetcar one evening on the way back to his apartment Mark rather clumsily asked me to marry him. Not the most romantic proposal I'll admit, but I said yes.

Shortly after our engagement, Mark suggested that we take a trip out of town to visit his family so that I could meet his parents. He didn't talk much about his family or his childhood; only that he had left home as soon as he was old enough to come to the 'big city'. I got the impression that there was something about his past that he felt ashamed of, but never managed to get to the bottom of it.

Mark's parents welcomed me into their home with open arms, and I got on really well with his mum. They lived on a working farm – not as farmers, but as caretakers of the farmhouse on behalf of the farm owners. It was almost the complete opposite to what I had expected, though I would have been hard-pressed to describe exactly what my expectations had been.

We spent a long weekend up there, and I was deliriously happy. I was able to forget about my anxiety over not fitting in but feeling that I needed to, and not knowing how I was going to pursue my love of design if I couldn't hold down a job for any decent amount of time. It was almost like I could be me (whoever me was becoming), even if just for a weekend. But the weekend was to take a slightly odd turn the afternoon before we left...

I was in the barn choosing a kitten to take back home with us as a gift for my roommate when Mark's mum came looking for me for a "chat". Instantly I started to hear warning bells and began to expect the worse, but her concerns turned out to be about Mark and not about me. She explained that he had suffered with severe depression and anxiety issues when he had lived at home but didn't go into any details as to why. She went on to explain that Mark had relied heavily on drugs to cope with his emotions and that had caused a rift to form between him and his father, that being the reason he had left home. When I asked her why she was telling me all this, she simply said that she was relying on me to take care of him.

At the time I didn't think much about it beyond it being a mother's concern for her son living away from home in a big city that she was ill at ease with. But later that conversation would come back to haunt me.

Shortly after our return to Toronto, cracks started to appear in Mark's façade, and I started to see the instability that his mother had warned me about. Mark would often comment that being a chef was one of the most stressful professions there is and that drug use in the industry was commonplace. Occasional recreational drug use wasn't out of the ordinary for me during that period of my life, but never anything more than a bit of fun at the weekends and never anything chemical. It was all strictly organic, aside from one three-day-long LSD trip that I swore I would never repeat as long as I lived. But Mark's drug use started to become more than just recreational and drifted into dependence. It wasn't long before his drug use was a daily occurrence, with him unable to go to work or be around other people while sober.

I started to express concern, and when my concern went unheeded our conversations rapidly deteriorated into arguments. After a few more months I felt I had no choice but to issue Mark with an ultimatum – clean up or lose me. I couldn't continue to watch him slowly unravel. I told him about what his mother had said to me and that the stress of trying to keep my promise to her was slowly driving me insane... the fact that I wasn't able to help him was more than I could bare.

Despite assurances that he was "in control" the drug use continued, and so I called off the engagement and effectively ended our relationship altogether.

Months past and I still saw Mark at the club. I was coldly civil if he spoke to me, but generally tried to avoid him as much as possible. I still harboured resentment towards him for putting me in the position of needing to choose between saving him or saving myself.

One evening, about a year after I had left, I was sitting on the steps outside Sanctuary getting some fresh air and chatting with one of the bouncers, when Mark walked up to me and asked if we could talk. Rather belligerently I said that we could talk right where we were and for him to just say what he had to say. A pleading look from him made the bouncers give us some privacy and he sat down on the ground opposite me.

Avoiding eye contact, Mark told me that he was leaving and that I would never have to see him again. To this day I don't remember what I said in reply or much of the conversation at all, except for the strange way that he pointed out the backpack he had with him and that I knew what the contents were. I recognised the bag as containing climbing equipment (rope, carabiners and such) that we had used to fashion a swing with in his parents' barn all those moons ago.

I don't recall how the conversation ended, just that it did and within hours had been forgotten.

Sanctuary was eventually shut down for getting busted selling alcohol to minors one too many times, and the die-hard regulars amongst us found new refuge in another club further uptown so unremarkable that I don't even remember its name.

I don't remember exactly how much time had passed, but sometime later, a mutual friend of both Mark and I, Andre, came looking for me at the club one night. While we were making our way outside to talk at a more comfortable volume, a passing acquaintance grabbed my arm and asked if I had heard that Mark was dead. Andre's reaction was immediate and aggressive, pushing the guy violently away with a look of pure venom. Instantly I knew something was very wrong and demanded to know what was going on. Andre turned and continued walking. It wasn't until we were outside that he turned to me and told me that it was true. Mark had been found dead by hikers in the middle of the woods in British Columbia – a province on the other side of the country, hanging from a tree. Police had ruled it a suicide.

I fell back against the wall like I had been punched in the stomach. I was utterly devastated! The memory of that last conversation on the steps of Sanctuary came rushing back with vivid clarity; all the tiny warning signs that I missed that night became painfully clear: the tone of his voice when he said I would never have to see him again; the way in which he pointed out the rucksack with his climbing gear in it; his body language and the fact that he never once made eye contact with me. The sudden inundation of emotions was too much for me take in and I ran back inside.

All the emotions that I was feeling at that instant for some reason decided to manifest themselves as anger, and in a fit of rage that is completely out of character for me I grabbed the acquaintance who had stopped us earlier by the front of his shirt and slammed him against a wall. "Don't ever speak to me again" I growled and then promptly stormed off. The rest of that night is a bit of a blur. I vaguely remember hiding in the ladies toilet for a while crying; someone coming to find me when the club was closing for the night; I have no recollection whatsoever of how I got home.

A few days later, Andre rang me to ask how I was doing. Then he braced me for more bad news. Apparently the police forensic photographs had been leaked and someone had posted them on Gore Gallery which was a website dedicated to showing real-life photos of death and violence. I think by telling me, Andre was hoping to avoid a repeat of the incident at the club of someone blurting out the news with no thought as to how it would affect me. He wanted me to hear it from him first hand. I asked if he had seen the pictures himself, and he admitted that he had but that it was best that I didn't. Apparently, it had been several days before Mark's body was discovered, during which time animals had got to him. Not a pleasant thought.

To this day I don't know what made me go and search for the photos. I think part of me was still clinging to the hope that it had all been a mistake, but it wasn't. Andre's description of how mutilated the body was had been wholly accurate; Mark's features were almost indistinguishable. If I hadn't recognised the medallion that he always wore, I could possibly convince myself that it wasn't him, but in the horrifying seconds that I glanced at the image I immediately knew it was. And that image will be burned into my memory for as long as I live.

I suffered with unbearable nightmares for months afterwards, and I blamed myself for years more, constantly berating myself for all the warning signs that I had missed. I felt that in some small way that I had driven him to hitchhike halfway across the country in an effort to run from his past until he could run no more and finally took his own life.

I didn't go to the funeral, and I have never visited his grave site. I was too afraid of coming face to face with Mark's mother and having to admit that I had let her down; that I had failed to take care of her son.

The few people who knew what had really happened between Mark and I tried to comfort me over the months and years that followed. Patiently reminding me that I did everything that I could for him at the time; that I could never have anticipated what was to come. Pointing out that I had no idea what manner of experiences he had in the months after he had left Toronto; that any number of things completely unrelated to what had transpired between us could have contributed to his suicide.

Slowly, over many years, their words gradually began to sink in. The pain never fully went away, but the guilt lessened just enough to allow me to forgive myself. One evening, I went down to the lake shore near my parents' house with the engagement ring that I had kept all those years. For the first time since learning what had happened to Mark, I spoke to him out loud as I wished I had done that last night I saw him. I told him all the things that I had wanted to say that I never got the chance to... that I was sorry, that I missed him, and that ultimately I forgave him. I then caste my engagement ring into the lake and said a final goodbye.

"I shouldn't have known better,
Because I couldn't have
known better,
Because I hadn't yet learnt
what I know now"

– Sandy Newbigging; author of Mind Detox

Lessons Learned

Mark's suicide is an experience that changed me forever; and still affects me to this day. Though many of my memories of Mark have started to fade over time, that last conversation is as vivid in my mind as if it had happened only yesterday. The unspeakable loss, pain and guilt that I felt that night learning of Mark's ultimate fate bubble back to the surface every time I hear of someone else's experience with suicide. While I have been writing this book, I watched the blockbuster film *A Star is Born* featuring Lady Gaga and Bradley Cooper. The final scene mirrored so closely what Mark must have experienced that fateful day in the woods that I was in tears for hours afterwards. It's an experience that far too many people are faced with – either as someone contemplating suicide or dealing with the aftermath of being someone left behind in the wake of a loved one's suicide. But if you have never had personal experience of suicide from either side of the equation, you can never truly understand.

If Mark's suicide and the resulting emotional turmoil that I experienced for years afterwards taught me anything that I can pass on to you, it's this... you need to forgive yourself for things learnt in hindsight.

They say that hindsight is a wonderful thing, but it can also be a double-edged sword. There are going to be times in your life when you look back on events in your past and ask yourself why did I do/say that, why did I make that decision instead of the 'right' one. The problem is that we only know after the fact what the 'right' decision should have been. In the moment, we can only base decisions on our world view at that point in time. You may not have all the facts, you may not be aware of underlying factors surrounding a situation, not to mention that you will be a different person in that moment compared to who you will be weeks, months or years later.

None of us is omnipotent; no one can predict the future with any certainty. There is no telling what lessons you will learn with the benefit of hindsight. Some will be pleasant revelations, others will be a stark reminder that we all make mistakes. However, every now and then, hindsight will reveal something that if you are not careful can eat you alive with guilt and remorse; like a death that you could have potentially prevented. In those circumstances, you need to learn to forgive yourself.

Forgiveness, especially of oneself, can be extremely difficult. There are usually so many conflicting emotions wrapped up in how we are feeling about a situation that it can be nearly impossible to see the wood from the trees. Generally, we are our own worst critic, and once you perceive that you have made a mistake, it can be difficult to see past the negative.

Being able to forgive yourself requires empathy, compassion, kindness and understanding. It also requires you to accept that forgiveness is a choice; and one that only you can make.

If you are struggling with the idea of self-forgiveness, maybe these tips might help:

1. **It's okay to feel guilty.** Emotions are our brain's way of communicating with us. Happiness tells us that we have found something positive. Sadness lets us know that we have lost something of significance. Guilt lets us know that our actions or behaviour contradict our values or beliefs of right and wrong. Experiencing guilt demonstrates that we are already on the path to forgiveness. Just remember that guilt and shame are completely different. Guilt has a purpose, shame does not, and it is not healthy for us.

2. **Admit your mistakes.** How many times have we blamed little things on something other than our own actions? You were late

"because of the trains", or your forgot mum's birthday present "because I was busy". Avoiding blame is a common occurrence, but not very helpful if you are struggling with forgiveness. Own up to your actions; ignoring a problem does not make it go away.

3. **Apologise.** An apology takes two forms: to yourself and to anyone else affected by your actions. We naturally want to mend the fences of a broken relationship or trust that has been damaged by our mistakes. The only way to do that correctly is to own up to your culpability, admit that it was your fault and apologise for your actions. Be open and listen to the other person's response, but don't pressurise or demand that they forgive you straightaway – if ever. Next, apologise to your self for the decisions that led you to make the mistake in the first place. Many mental health professionals advocate writing yourself an apology letter to help you to externalise your feelings effectively and safely. Be sure to acknowledge that this error does not define you and remember to be kind to yourself – self-flagellation accomplishes nothing.

4. **Take care of yourself, mentally and physically.** Because guilt is such an intense,

visceral emotion, it can manifest itself in all sorts of ways. If you endure it for too long, it can start to impact on your mental and physical health in more serious ways such as depression, self-isolation and loss of confidence. You can also start to experience anxiety, tension headaches and lack of focus or concentration. If you're having problems moving forward, seek help from a therapist or healthcare professional.

5. **Be patient.** This is the hardest part, but also the most important. When we feel embarrassed or guilty, we just want things to go back to normal as quickly as possible. But you can't rush emotions – yours or anyone else's. Be patient and let things take their course.

Forgiveness is also a hallmark of a growth mindset. It is the ability to be able to grow, develop and adapt to changing situations, and learn from our mistakes. We are all human, with all the fallibilities that come with it. As humans we are never going to be perfect, we are never going to always make the right decision. As long as you are able to acknowledge that fact and choose to learn from your mistakes instead of dwelling on them, you will eventually find peace; even if it takes a while to get there.

"Forgive yourself first. Release the need to replay a negative situation over and over again in your mind. Don't become a hostage to your past by always reviewing and reliving your mistakes. Don't remind yourself of what should have, could have, or would have been. Release it and let it go."

– *Les Brown; American author & motivational speaker*

FIVE:

Things unsaid

*A*s you might have gathered by now, my relationship with boys was quite hit and miss during my youth; and in some cases downright tumultuous. But there was one relationship that forever sits head and shoulders above the rest (except for the one with my husband of course) – and the funny thing is we never actually dated.

My first Halloween at Sanctuary, I met someone who would play a major part in my life for years to come, and that was Greg.

Despite the lyrics from the goth anthem *Every Day is Halloween* by Ministry, Halloween was always a very special night at Sanctuary. Not only was every club regular in attendance, usually in full costume, but numbers were also inflated by a swell of 'normals' wanting to dance with the devil on All Hallows' Eve. It made for a packed house and sometimes tensions ran high. It was an unwritten rule that club regulars were not to be trifled with, and that particular night I witnessed the full meaning of that rule.

I was dancing to one of my favourite songs, *Love Cats* by The Cure, when I was elbowed quite hard in the ribs by an outsider who had decided that moshing on a packed goth club dance floor was the thing to do. Before I had a chance to catch my breath a number of bouncers and club regulars grabbed the offending miscreant by the collar and unceremoniously ejected him from the club, banning him from ever returning. Back in those days, justice was always swift and usually accompanied by threats of exceptional violence.

Soon afterwards, one of the regulars who had offered an enthusiastic hand in booting the little mosher from the club came up to me and asked if I was OK. He wasn't very tall, only slightly taller than me, wearing a black leather biker jacket adorned with numerous chains and sporting a red mohawk. He carried an ornate ebony cane and wore a mischievous smile. He introduced himself as Greg and invited me across the street to grab a coffee at the 24hr coffee shop so that we could chat at a more reasonable volume.

I found him absolutely fascinating! Greg proved to be highly intelligent and a great conversationalist. We talked about philosophy, politics, the social impact and position of goth culture, even religion. I discovered that he was a life-long student of unarmed combat and mixed martial arts; hence the graceful ease with which he had assisted in ejecting that metal-headed miscreant from the club earlier that evening. Before I knew it, my friends who I had arrived with were looking for me to go home; three hours had passed in what felt like moments.

Greg was one of the original regulars at Sanctuary, and as such I felt was miles out of my league, but despite that he made a point of coming over and talking to me anytime he saw me at the club. I discovered that he lived not far from my college campus, and we soon started hanging out during the day whenever I had a break from lectures and when his route as a bike courier brought him to the neighbourhood. Greg had even been the person who introduced me to Mark.

A very close bond started to form between Greg and I. Despite the fact that we were both hanging out at a club that catered for outsiders, neither of us were like the rest of the club's frequent patrons. Greg only worked as a bike courier in order to save up for his Masters degree, and we both held interests outside of just the club. Deep down, we both knew that we would eventually move beyond that place but would still savour every minute of it while it lasted.

It wasn't long before things between Greg and I became physical as well as intellectual, but for some strange reason it never really went any further than casual sex while we were both single – which for him was all the time. Despite being the subject of lust by pretty much every woman (and even some of the men) at Sanctuary, I don't ever recall Greg being in a committed relationship with anyone. We genuinely enjoyed each other's company in whatever form that took depending on what the circumstances were at that given moment in time. We were the quintessential example of 'best friends with benefits'.

I grew to rely on Greg's judgement, advice, and discretion for a great many things. He even became a protector of sorts, shielding me from some of the more disreputable elements of Toronto's underground culture. He always seemed to appear at the right place at the right time to get me out of trouble; whether it be an over-enthusiastic ex or some crackpot cornering me in the park thinking I would be easy prey. As he put it, he was passionately loyal to his friends and merciless with their enemies.

Shortly before Mark's death, Greg moved from Toronto to Ottawa to start his Masters degree in international politics, which also included a study term in Russia, so I didn't see very much of him after that. However, whenever he was in town, we made a point of seeing each other as much as possible. On one such trip, Greg suggested that it would be great if I came out to Ottawa to stay with him for spring break.

That trip ended up being an amazing week that I remember fondly to this day. Greg showed me around all the attractions of Ottawa that he knew I would enjoy – the Canadian history museum, the penny markets, even Ottawa's own version of Sanctuary across the river in Hull. There was a level of intimacy between us that I had never really felt before, either with him or anyone else before him; one that was physical, emotional, and intellectual all at once. He also seemed different in Ottawa than he had been in Toronto, more relaxed and at peace with himself and with his direction in life. It seemed that without the scrutiny of everyone else from the club, we could finally just be ourselves.

The final day of my trip, I remember standing with Greg at the window of his apartment, saying goodbye before I had to leave to catch my bus back home. I had always harboured really strong feelings for Greg ever since one particular night when he had whispered something to me in Russian that just made me melt. He never did translate what he had said that night, but I never felt the same about him after it.

I never expressed those feelings to Greg for fear that he would reject the idea of anything more permanent between us – why would he date me if he had the choice of anyone at Sanctuary he wanted? But at that moment, I desperately wanted to tell him how I felt; that I didn't want to leave and would happily give up my life in Toronto to be with him. I could feel that there was something between us, something more than just enjoying each other's company, but in the end, I bottled it. I was too afraid of ruining the amazing friendship that we had to take a chance. So, I got on the bus and went back home.

As circumstances would have it, that was the last opportunity I ever had to tell Greg how I really felt. Our lives diverged in very opposite directions after that. It would be decades later and oceans apart before I got the chance to tell him what I had wanted to say that day. The irony was that it turned out he had wanted to tell me nearly the very same thing. The reason why he didn't was that he didn't think I would give up the life I had at Sanctuary and leave all my friends behind for an uncertainty. If only either one of us had had the courage to speak our mind, our lives could have been very different – especially mine as you will soon learn.

Quite often I find myself thinking back to that weekend and wondering "what if"? Where would a life in Ottawa have taken me? Would it have even worked between Greg and I? One thing is for certain; I would have avoided a lot of the pain and torment that was to follow.

"There is no security on this earth; there is only opportunity."

– Douglas MacArthur; American general

Lessons Learned

I have no doubt that everyone has similar sorts of stories somewhere in their past. It may not be surrounding an unexpressed declaration of love, but there is always a feeling of regret of not saying or doing something when presented with the opportunity.

The lesson that I learned from not taking the opportunity to express how I felt to Greg when I had the chance was that you should always take these opportunities when they present themselves; you never know when/if you will ever have the opportunity again. And in situations where that opportunity doesn't come back around, you are inevitably going to experience a sense of regret and a litany of "what ifs".

As you will read in the coming chapters, my life after that trip to Ottawa took a dark and dangerous turn for the worse. There has rarely been a time when I've looked back on the preceding years of my life and thought, "What if I had said something to Greg that day, I might have avoided all the pain and turmoil that followed altogether". Thoughts like that can really eat away at you.

As luck would have it, the life that I have lived, despite the dark few years that followed that trip, has been amazing. I finally met the love of my life, got married, and started my own business; and I wouldn't trade any of those experiences for the world.

Likewise, I know that the life Greg has lived has been equally amazing for him. Meeting the love of his life, getting married, having his beautiful daughter and a distinguished career as a captain in the Canadian Army, with all the passions and adventures that went with it, are all things that I know he wouldn't trade for anything either.

But all that can only be seen in hindsight. In the moment, you never know what the future may hold. It could easily have all gone another way, and that one opportunity for an idyllic life in Ottawa could have been my only opportunity at happiness. Because you never know, you should be willing to take risks, albeit calculated ones, to ensure that you don't live a life of regret.

As I have mentioned in the previous chapter, we are human, and we all make mistakes. There are going to be times where you work up the courage to say or do something and it's going to be the wrong call. But we only get one chance at life; there are no replays, there is no pause button. It is better to take the shot and miss than to never play the game.

"I'd rather regret the things I've done than regret the things I haven't done."

– Lucille Ball; American comedian

SIX:

"I don't know my own strength"

2001 was a turning point year for me. It was the year that I gained true independence and faced the world on my own. Prior to 2001, I had made several failed attempts at living on my own, usually in increasingly dodgy basement apartments in downtown Toronto, sometimes with friends and sometimes on my own. It was never long before Mum would say that I really needed to come home for fear of me turning into a hermit from lack of sunlight or any other number of unwholesome reasons. But 2001 was different, as Mum and Dad took the decision to move back to the UK.

Dad had rather suddenly found himself out of work after being made redundant from a job he had held for over 15 years, and was struggling to find new employment. After an exploratory trip to the UK on his own to investigate the job market there, they made the decision that relocation was their best option.

I gave serious consideration to going with them, but I had finally found a job as a designer that I really enjoyed, working for a company that designed titles and end credits for movies and which I felt had potential to further my career in graphic design. After much debate, and even more sleepless nights, I decided that I was going to stay and get my own place. Mum reluctantly agreed, but on the condition that she would help me find an apartment that SHE found suitable. We eventually settled on a 2nd floor apartment on Bathurst Street, and I moved in about a month before Mum and Dad were due to leave.

Life in my new apartment as an independent woman started out well enough. To help with the rent, I shared the apartment with my then boyfriend Steve, and everything was going smoothly. I finally felt like a proper grown-up!

Not long after my parents moved, Steve brought home a friend he had met at the local occult shop; a little hole-in-the-wall place down the street from us that sold pagan books and other curiosities. He was handsome, funny, exceedingly charming and appeared to not have a care in the world. It wasn't long before he was spending quite a bit of time with us, coming over for dinner several times a week, and occasionally crashing on our couch.

Over time Steve became increasingly jealous of the time and attention that I was paying to our new friend; a jealousy that in my opinion was completely unfounded and bordered on being ridiculous. Little did I know at the time that my opinion wasn't really my own and that my position on the matter was being carefully manipulated.

You may have noticed by now that I am not mentioning this particular person's name, and that is a conscious decision that you will understand shortly. For now, just accept that I will never use his name and will refer to him simply as Mr. X.

My relationship with Steve gradually deteriorated, and he eventually moved out when it became apparent that I would take Mr. X's side in most arguments that arose between us. This suddenly left me with rent to pay on my own which, despite my well-paid job at Film Effects, I couldn't afford. Unsurprisingly, Mr. X "reluctantly" offered to move into the spare bedroom to help me to cover the bills.

No sooner had Mr. X moved in, the charm offensive *really* started, and before I knew it I was being swept off my feet in a whirlwind romance. He became a knight in shining armour overnight; opening doors for me, lavishing me with compliments and gifts, and generally treating me like a princess. But it wasn't to last.

Looking back on that time, I can't really pinpoint when things started to change or even when I *noticed* that they had changed, but at some point, they had. It was a gradual, subtle process; seemingly innocent accidents caused by a play fight getting too rough resulted in bruises; a voice raised and then quickly apologised for. Each incident was quickly followed by the reassurance that "I would never intentionally hurt you" or "I'm so sorry, I just don't know my own strength sometimes" or "I didn't mean to yell, I'm just stressed about xyz". All the while, the 'knight in shining armour' routine continued, convincing me that the excuses must be genuine.

Over time, the excuses started to change, and blame began to shift to me instead of him. "I would never intentionally hurt you" shifted to "Look what you made me do", or "I didn't mean to yell" started to become "You've brought it on yourself" and eventually "You're just getting what you deserve".

Mr. X also started to severely restrict my movements and access to friends, though I didn't really work this out until years later. He would take my phone and go through my call or text history and lash out with angry questions when he spotted unknown numbers or any name which wasn't female. He started following me whenever I left the house; a habit I was not aware of until the first time I deviated from my declared destination, which drew immediate and severe repercussions.

He began to dictate all areas of our lives, from food to finance, social circles to sex, and I was never allowed to say "no" to any of it. Refusing to do anything that he said or to attempt to contradict him resulted in severe verbal, mental, and sometimes physical, abuse. My brain has mercifully "forgotten" many of the specifics, but I do recall being hit across the jaw with a cordless phone; having a cigarette put out on my thigh; and countless occasions of being thrown against walls or to the floor.

***

Throughout my life, I have heard countless stories on the news of women remaining in abusive relationships, with people inevitably asking the question, "Why did they stay?" The answer is that when you are in the middle of it, you just don't realise that what is happening IS abuse. 90% of the 'abuse' in these situations is psychological; it's the gradual dismantling of everything that makes you an individual. This turns you into whatever the abuser wants you to be to them. You begin to believe the excuses and the lies; that you truly are getting what you deserve and that you are not worthy of anything more than what you get. It's brainwashing to an extent that would make a Cold War CIA operative green with envy, pure and simple.

It also usually happens gradually over a period of time, and more often than not after a period of profound bliss when that person has been 'perfect' to you in every way. You accept the initial apologies and excuses because you remember them being so perfect, that this sudden behaviour HAS to be a mistake or an accident; it has to be your fault and not theirs.

By the time you wake up and reality sets in, it's too late. Any willpower or independent thinking you may have possessed previously has been beaten out of you – either figuratively or worse still, literally. Your life becomes all about maintaining calm and avoiding confrontation at all costs for fear of the repercussions.

That is the reality of abuse.

"Prepare for the worst but hope for the best – the former makes you sensible, and the latter makes you an optimist."

– *Dale Carnegie; American writer & lecturer*

Lessons Learned

As traumatic as this period of my life was, there are several powerful lessons that I learned from my experiences. The first is, never assume the worst won't ever happen to you.

Remember those stories on the news I mentioned? You never expect that one day that could be you. From the outside looking in, you always think that you will have the clarity of thought to avoid situations like that in the first place or prevent them from ever going that far. I certainly did – that is until I found myself stuck in the middle of that very same situation, completely unaware of how I had got there.

There's a saying that Dad always used to say to me growing up – expect the worse and hope for the best. I know that he meant it as a way of planning for everyday mundane things like packing for a trip, but it is super-applicable to life in general.

Any new situation you find yourself in, or any large decision that you need to make, think to yourself, "What is the absolute worse-case scenario?" If all hell were to break loose, what is the worst that can happen? You then plan for it. Even if it's just in the back of your mind, have a contingency plan of what you could do to get yourself out of the situation. You can then carry on with the situation or decision, putting your heart, soul, and energy into making it the best decision or situation possible – which is the hoping for the best part of the saying.

It's by using this principle that I even had the nerve to date again, let alone settle down and get married. Do I fear the past repeating itself? Sometimes. The scars (both physical and mental) run deep from that time of my life, and I will probably never be 100% free from them. To this day, I still have triggers that will instantly send me back to that time in my memory. I can't even be in the vicinity of someone raising their voice in anger without it freaking me out, regardless of whether that voice has been raised at me or not, and I'm far more nervous than most people about fire in the hands of someone else. But I have learned to trust myself that I won't become a victim again, because I now know that it CAN happen to anyone and I have prepared myself accordingly for it.

The second main lesson that I learned from my experience with Mr. X is to never ignore the warning signs.

I strongly believe in the principle of 'cause and effect'. Nothing in this world happens out of the blue, without warning. There is always a cause for any event or situation; something that leads up to it happening. The problem is that, most of the time, these causes are so small that we either miss them or ignore them.

Ignoring the warning signs in any situation can be a dangerous game. Brushing off something as being trivial or isolated is fine if it IS only trivial or isolated. If it starts to become a pattern or starts to escalate even a little, you need to pay attention – the Universe is trying to tell you something.

Looking back on my time with Mr. X, the early part of that situation is LITTERED with dozens of repeated and escalating warning signs that I chose to ignore in favour of the vision that he had portrayed of himself in the very beginning. I wanted so desperately to believe that he WAS a knight in shining armour that I was blind to all the rust and scratches that started to appear on that armour as our relationship progressed.

Don't ignore the warning signs, and take appropriate action (from your worst-case scenario contingency) before the situation progresses to the point when it is too late.

Now I, more than most, fully appreciate just how hard a lesson that is to live by. Despite my experience with Mr. X, I still find myself making mistakes because I've missed a warning sign along the way. The trick is to not ignore the warning signs that you do see and to react straightaway. The most appropriate reaction may be to just be more vigilant and to look for a recurring pattern, because you don't want to overreact to a one-off.

Most importantly, don't be afraid to act. Domestic violence is a huge problem in modern society, but unfortunately it is also one that carries with it a disproportionate amount of perceived shame. According to the Office of National Statistics (ONS), about 800,000 men and 1.3 million women suffered domestic abuse in England and Wales during 2018[1] – that's over two million cases in a single year! You are NOT alone, and you have nothing to be ashamed of. So, if the warning signs are there no matter how minor, do something about it! Confide in someone you trust or reach out to one of the anonymous abuse hotlines. If you genuinely feel in danger, contact the police.

---

1. "Domestic abuse in England and Wales – Office for National Statistics". www.ons.gov.uk. Retrieved 2019-03-09

"The turnings of life seldom
show a signpost; or rather,
the sign is always there, it is
usually placed some distance
back, like the notices that
give warning of a bad hill or
a level railway-crossing."

– *Edith Wharton; 19th century novelist*

SEVEN:

Rose-tinted glasses won't change the world

*L*ike countless teenagers around the world, I did my fair share of experimenting with drugs during my college years. Nearly all my dabblings in narcotics were restricted to the herbal varieties. I tried hallucinogenic mushrooms on a couple of occasions, but they were hard to come by during that time in Toronto, so my experiences with those were few and far between. I had my drink spiked with peyote (which is an hallucinogen derived from cactus plants) at a club one evening. Although that wasn't exactly deliberate, it was an interesting experience watching the bathmat in my boyfriend's apartment crawl up the wall, across the ceiling, into the bathtub and back out again onto the floor while I was going to the toilet.

I did experiment with chemical drugs once. Mark (remember him from Chapter 4?) asked me one weekend if I wanted to take an acid (LSD) trip with him. It was only going to be the two of us alone for three days, so it was the safest time to experiment with it. I had never tried it before, but for Mark it was a common drug to take. I remember that weekend vividly. We ended up taking two doses each because the first dose didn't seem to do anything. Classic mistake! A few hours later, both doses hit like a train and I remember being high as a kite for two days straight. I think that because of my experiences in the past with mushrooms, and the peyote incident, the intense hallucinations that accompanied the acid trip didn't bother me, and so I just relaxed into it and went along for the ride. However, I was not in any way prepared for the experience of 'coming down' off LSD, which was extremely painful and profoundly unpleasant. To the point that I swore I would never touch the stuff again no matter how fun the trip had been.

My drug of choice (if you could call it that) was marijuana. I was introduced to it at a house party during my senior year at high school. Everyone was taking a toke and then passing it onto the next person. I tried to resist, saying no each time it came to my turn, which thankfully everyone was cool with. It wasn't so much peer pressure that got me to relent and try it later on that evening with the owners of the house who were my close friends at the time; it was seeing everyone else having such a great time on it and no one being affected by any of the "bad" things that I had been told about weed by authority figures and the media.

At that time in Toronto, weed was cheap and easy to get hold of. Though it was a Class C drug under the letter of the law, the police would more than likely just confiscate it (usually for their own use off-duty) than actually charge you with an offence. So, it was somewhat safe from a legal point of view as long as you didn't have too much on you. I never once had a bad experience with it, and quite enjoyed the way it relaxed any outside noise and tension and allowed my mind to explore ideas. It would often end up producing the typical "right the world's wrongs" type of scenes you see in the movies.

Now, don't get me wrong, I was not a 'stoner' by any stretch of the imagination. I would have an occasional joint with friends on the odd weekend here and there if it was available. We'd sit around, eating junk food and talk about history, philosophy, politics, or any other profound subject that piqued our interest at the time. Harmless, teenage indulgences.

However, during my time with Mr. X, that all changed.

Marijuana was a common pastime for Mr. X, often consisting of several joints a week. Unsurprisingly, as a result of his liking of the drug, it meant that it was something that I was expected to participate in each and every time.

I have a suspicion that he saw it as a way of keeping me docile and compliant. Which it did. As a result, the yelling and abuse was considerably less when I was high. Naturally, when I noticed the connection, I started to want it more and more often, which Mr. X dutifully provided.

At its peak, I alone was consuming 3-4 joints a DAY, which equated to around half an ounce a week. Soon, all our rent and most of our food money was going on marijuana. We were evicted from my nice two-bedroom apartment for non-payment of rent and proceeded to move from house to house in ever-seedier neighbourhoods. Each time staying just long enough before the landlord would kick us out. Eventually it got to the point where we started growing it in small batches in our spare bedroom wardrobe for the times when we couldn't afford to buy it.

For me, marijuana was an escape from the reality of my world. It stopped the noise and the violence, even if only for a few hours. It allowed me to relax, and it took away the pain of any injuries I might have at any given time. I was able to retreat into a secret world in my head which became the only place where I felt safe. It made me no longer care that I didn't have a voice or a will of my own; it was just easier that way.

***

The reality was that I was an addict. And though everyone who smokes weed says that it is a harmless drug, the significant amount of it that I consumed during that time has had an ongoing adverse effect on me. I have since developed a mild stammer when I'm stressed and an inability to think of the correct words when under pressure. I have huge gaps in my memory from before that period in my life where I can no longer remember specific details. That has proved challenging while writing this book! And in rare occasions of extreme stress I can find myself in a trance-like state, conscious of what is going on around me but somehow detached from it.

That last side-effect has at times proved to be a blessing in disguise. One incident that I can recall was when I experienced my first severe panic attack and ended up in A&E. The trance-like state (which came out of nowhere) proved to be the only thing that calmed me down enough for the nurses to administer an IV line.

"Addictions ... started out like magical pets, pocket monsters. They did extraordinary tricks, showed you things you hadn't seen, were fun. But came, through some gradual dire alchemy, to make decisions for you. Eventually, they were making your most crucial life-decisions. And they were ... less intelligent than goldfish."

– **Zero History** *by William Gibson, Viking 02/09/2010*

Lessons Learned

The lessons that can be learned from any addiction, whether it be alcohol, drugs, gambling, sex, whatever, are always profound and usually revolve around themes of excess and controlling desires. However, the lesson that I learned from the experience was this: altering perception doesn't alter reality.

Like many addicts, my reliance on marijuana was intended to help me to escape from the reality of the situation that I found myself in. I honestly believed that by altering my perception of what was going on around me I could somehow escape it, even if only for the short time while the high lasted.

The reality is that no matter how much I tried to change my perception of my situation, it was always exactly the same when I sobered up. Nothing changed. And I think this has a profound implication on some aspects of modern attitudes to mental health.

There are now so many alternative, holistic, and new-age approaches to mental health – some of which are fairly mainstream – that talk about altering your perception of an event or situation in order to have a more positive experience or relationship with it. I'm all for therapies and treatments that help us to find balance and peace with our memories and emotions in a natural way, without having to resort to drugs (pharmaceutical or otherwise). However, I do have one big caveat: that you never lose sight of the fact that the reality of a situation or an event is REAL, and no amount of altered perception will change that fact.

By all means, alter your perception of a situation or event to help you cope better with it. But remember that it won't alter the *reality* of that situation or event. So, use the greater peace or confidence you gain from your altered perception to *change* the reality but don't just hide in the altered perception hoping that the situation or event will change itself. It won't.

And if you are using drugs or alcohol to change your perception of your reality, take it from me that it is never worth it. The side-effects of what you are doing to yourself, no matter how imperceptible they may appear now, will catch up with you one day and will not be worth the temporary relief you receive in the moment.

Thankfully I was able to kick my addiction to marijuana on my own without any outside support, and have been completely clean ever since. I go into how I managed that in a later chapter. But if you find yourself unable to manage an addiction, please seek help. Talk to someone you trust: a friend, family member, your doctor, a therapist. Get the help you need to not only manage but beat your addiction so that it doesn't end up managing or beating you.

"Imagination should be used, not to escape reality but to create it."

– Colin Wilson; writer & philosopher

EIGHT:

Bridges

2003 ended up being a landmark year that would change my life forever. But you would never have guessed it from the way it started out.

Though I don't have any specific memories from the start of that year, I know something had started to change. Some little seed of recognition that the path my life was on was not quite right must have started to germinate. I started to see that what Mr. X was doing to me wasn't what I 'deserved', that I didn't bring it all on myself, but I couldn't see any way out. He still had a vice-like grip on my willpower. And as a result, depression started to sink in.

I felt hopelessness about the reality of my situation. I was slowly starting to realise that it was wrong, but could see no means of escape. Mr. X's systematic dismantling of who I used to be was complete; everything of the person

I had been seemed dead or from a time so far away that it was irretrievable.

I started to walk through life like a half-dead zombie. Mindlessly moving from one task to the next, only paying enough attention to avoid aggravating my situation any further. For the most part I stopped eating, only having meagre bits and pieces here and there to prevent my passing out, and as a result started to lose frightening amounts of weight.

The only animation coming into my life were during my weekly catch-up calls with Mum. Never over Skype, as they had been when they first moved away; now reserved only for over the phone so she couldn't see the reality that I had carefully hidden from my parents week-on-week for nearly two years.

2003 started very cold in Toronto, but with little snow. Everything was frozen, but not buried as it had been many years previously and since. February 14th of that year was no exception: cold, overcast, but with no snow or ice on the streets. Despite the weed-induced haze that surrounds everything else from that period of my life, I remember February 14th, 2003 all too vividly.

I was on the bus – alone – I don't completely recall where I was going or for what purpose. It suddenly dawned on me that it was Valentine's Day, and for some reason that realisation was more than I could bare. Tears started to roll down my cheeks and I felt so utterly alone – an island of one on a nearly packed bus of 50-60 other passengers. I had to escape! The sea of unsuspecting and uncaring humanity that surrounded me was more than I could handle.

The very next stop, I got off, not even caring where I was or whatever my original task had been. As fate would have it, I had got off the bus at Bathurst St and St Clair, just a few blocks from the idyllic little apartment that I had lived in with Steve when my parents first left for the UK. Recognising where I was felt like a twisting of the knife in my heart, recalling how blissful life had been a scant 2 years ago and just how much had changed in me since.

I started walking, not really knowing where I was walking to, or even really caring – I just needed to be doing something, moving somewhere, for fear that the world would suddenly crash in on me if I stood still too long. Next thing I know, I'm standing on the Bathurst St bridge looking over the frozen Cedarvale Ravine.

The river at the bottom of that ravine is not very deep, but it's fairly fast. Normally it never freezes in winter, but this particular year had been colder than normal, and there was a thin layer of rippled ice across its entire width. The Bathurst St bridge stands about 100ft above the ravine that forms one of the numerous green belts that criss-cross the city. But the bridge is old and the 100ft drop is only protected by a narrow 4ft concrete barrier, not the 6ft retaining fence more common on modern bridges.

I stopped and look over the edge, not seeing the river but seeing an abyss instead. A quiet, peaceful abyss. I start hearing Mr. X's voice in my head, repeating over and over again all the insults and verbal abuse that he had ever said to me... "You're not worthy of anything", "No one else would put up with you", "You're only getting exactly what you deserve", "You brought this all on yourself", "Even your parents don't want you", "You're of no use to anyone".

I shut my eyes tight and put my hands over my ears, hoping to block out the words that I knew were only inside my head. And suddenly it stopped with a final shout: "No one would miss you if you died".

Everything else was silence after that. I couldn't hear the cars driving past on the street behind me, nor the voices of any passing pedestrians. Just the fading echo of that last fatal statement.

I looked over into the abyss again and started to climb up onto the edge of the concrete barrier, thinking of nothing else but the fact that it would soon all be over; cold, yes, but quiet. Once I got my footing and looked down again, I didn't see the abyss, but the jagged, razor sharp ice over the river... and suddenly I saw my mother's face. Warm, comforting, protective; the way she always looked when I woke up from a nightmare and went running to my parents' bedroom as a child.

The reality of what I was about to do hit me like a splash of ice water from the frozen river below! I couldn't do this... not to her, no matter how bad things were!!!

I quickly jumped down from the barrier and ran back to the bus stop. Thankfully, I didn't have to wait long for the bus I wanted. I got on, and sat staring out the window, dumbfounded by what had just happened. But I didn't go home. Instead, I realised that I needed help, and I wasn't going to get it at home. So, I went to CAMH Mental Hospital on Queen Street.

With tears streaming down my cheeks, I haltingly tried to explain to the nurse on reception what had just happened. The nurse very pointedly asked me if I was still a threat to myself, and when I replied no, told me to take a seat in the waiting room. After I had removed my coat, she asked me when had been the last time I had had something to eat.

I remember sitting in the waiting room, feeling a strange feeling of safety for the first time in an awfully long time. I started to secretly hope that my ordeal was finally over, and a way out was about to open up in front of me.

Unfortunately, this was not the case. After what felt like hours, I was 'examined' by the on-call psychiatrist, which primarily consisted of asking me about my current state of mind and nothing about what had brought me to this situation in the first place. The interview then quickly concluded with the psychiatrist stating that I was no longer viewed as a threat to myself or society and was therefore released. They called me a taxi and sent me home.

In fairness to the staff at CAMH, I didn't particularly offer any details about my true situation. As ever, I was fearful that somehow every word I said would get back to Mr. X and provoke more anger and violence. Maybe if I had had the courage to speak up, things might have been different, but this was not to be the occasion for that. So, I dutifully went back home to endure whatever punishment was in store for me for the stupidity of what I had done.

"To be, or not to be:
that is the question:
Whether 'tis nobler in
the mind to suffer
The slings and arrows of
outrageous fortune,
Or to take arms against
a sea of troubles,
And by opposing end
them? To die: to sleep;

No more; and by a
sleep to say we end
The heart-ache and the
thousand natural shocks
That flesh is heir to, 'tis
a consummation
Devoutly to be wish'd"

— *William Shakespeare – Hamlet, Act III, Scene I*

Lessons Learned

The lesson I learned from that fateful day in February 2003, was at once simple but also profound. No matter how alone you may feel, no matter how bad things get, *someone* will always miss you.

You would think, after my experience with Mark's suicide, that the thought of doing it myself would never cross my mind. But it did, and so I can fully understand what can drive a person to feel that there is no other way out. That there is no other solution, and that the world would be either better off without you or that no one would care if you were no longer there. I get it! But there is always a different path through the maze; there is always a solution, and there is always someone who will care that you're no longer around.

Sometimes the crisis you feel stuck in is the result of a conflict with those very people who you would normally rely on for support, such as your family or a partner. Even in these situations the conflict never warrants the loss of your life; no matter how bitter the conflict is at the time. Believe me, they would never want that to happen to you.

So how do you get out?

By our very nature, humans are pack animals. Just like wolves and horses, our mental and emotional wellbeing is improved by meaningful interactions with other members of our pack (our family, friends and partners). Isolation from the rest of the pack (whether genuine or imagined) can have all sorts of negative effects on our state of mind.

The isolation that we feel because of our circumstances is usually also the same gilded cage that prevents us from seeking help. Isolation has a tendency of breeding fear; fear that no one will understand or care, fear that we are overreacting, or fear of the repercussions.

Most people in any form of crisis never fully appreciate the network of people that are available to help. From friends and family, to medical professionals, to support organisations like The Samaritans and The Red Cross, even churches regardless of whether you are religious or not, all will offer aid where possible.

Asking for help is hard, yes – even harder when you already feel a burden to those around you, but it is not a sign of weakness. On the contrary, the courage to ask for help is a sign of strength, determination, and character. It shows that you are brave enough to admit your fallibilities and seek support in overcoming them.

No matter how dark your world may appear, there is always someone pure of heart who would do anything to help someone in need, stranger or not. So never feel that you are alone, and never feel that no one will care if you live or die.

Find the courage to break through the fear and reach out for help.

"Regardless of what challenge you are facing right now, know that it has not come to stay. It has come to pass. During these times, do what you can with what you have, and ask for help if needed. Most importantly, never surrender. Put things in perspective. Take care of yourself. Find ways to replenish your energy, strengthen your faith and fortify yourself from the inside out."

– Les Brown; motivational speaker & author

NINE:

Living with a stranger

After the events in February, things pretty much went back to normal, at least on the outside. Inside my head a war was brewing between my conscious mind and the little voice that was gradually getting louder and louder, telling me that everything about my situation was wrong.

One morning in mid-August something in my brain finally snapped. My conscious mind finally woke up to the truth, that the little voice was right. I realised that I needed to get out or it was going cost me my life, either by my own hand or his.

I don't remember there being a final straw that led to this realisation. There was no final threat, no one strike too many, just a calm awakening to the truth that enough was finally enough.

At the time, I was working a meagre part-time job at a storage solutions store in the local mall. It involved me talking to other people, but Mr. X was convinced that only other women would visit a shop like that and so it was allowed, as long as my pay was made in cash and handed over to him for "safe-keeping".

That day I left for my shift as normal, but on the 20-minute bus ride I formulated a desperate plan...

When I arrived at work, instead of starting my shift I asked my boss if we could have a quick private conversation before we opened the store. She agreed, and I proceeded to tell her everything – the mental and physical abuse, the threats, even my brush with suicide. I finished by saying that I was profoundly sorry, but that I needed to leave.

I really didn't know what I was expecting to happen. I had only been working there for a few months, and I had made little-to-no effort to get to know anyone that I worked with or to open up in any way. To this day I cannot remember my boss's name or even recall her face, but I will never forget what she did next. She paid me 2 weeks' wages straight out of the till and told me I could leave right then and there. She said that if he came by the store looking for me, she would lie, saying that I had never shown up for work that day.

Feeling both shocked and encouraged by the fact that someone had believed me, let alone was willing to help me, I went to the central bus station with the plan of catching the next Greyhound bus cross-country to

Newfoundland to stay with my grandmother. But while I was standing in line at the ticket office something made me think that I should ring my parents then and there and let them know what was going on instead of waiting until I was safely away.

I didn't go into any specifics over the phone, just that things had got out of hand with Mr. X, that I didn't feel safe, and that I was going to stay with Grandma. With the calm efficiency that Dad always exhibits in a crisis, he told me instead to go to the Royal York hotel downtown and to ring them back when I got there. "By the time you ring us back, we will have a plan."

Despite the strain that our relationship had been through when I was a difficult teenager, I always trusted Dad completely. I knew that if he said he would have a plan by the time I made it across town to the Royal York, then he would move heaven and earth to make that true. 20 minutes later, I dutifully called Dad back from the Royal York's opulent lobby – one of the most prestigious hotels in Toronto.

He proceeded to tell me that he had been in contact with Steve and Maureen; close family friends who lived about an hour away from me. They had agreed to come and pick me up and take me to stay with them until a flight could be arranged for me to the UK; I was going to go home.

I started to panic a little at the thought of having to wait for at least an hour (maybe more depending on traffic into the city) to be rescued; in that time, he could find me. Dad reassured me that I was in probably the safest building in all of Toronto. Royalty, presidents, billionaires and industry tycoons stayed in this hotel when visiting Toronto; security would not allow anything to happen to me. He told me to have a quiet word with the concierge to explain that I was being followed and needed somewhere safe to wait for someone to come and get me.

I had my doubts but trusted Dad's judgement and did as he instructed. To my surprise, the staff at the hotel were amazing. They sat me in a quiet corner of the lobby in full sight of the main reception desk. They brought me a coffee, and someone was assigned to keep an eye on me at all times. True to their word, an hour later Steve and Maureen walked through the door. I felt so relieved to see them that I ran straight to Maureen and started crying.

After I collected myself a little, we started to walk back to their car. Once safely inside, Maureen turned to me and, as gently as she could, informed me that Dad had given them very specific instructions that before going home they were to take me to the nearest police station to make a statement and ask for an escort to collect a few belongings from the apartment – mainly my passport, so that I could actually fly. Immediately the panic started to set in again – I couldn't make an official statement. Telling one or two people was one thing but THIS was just too much.

I suspect that Maureen had expected such a reaction, and more than likely so had Dad, which is why he had asked them to do it no matter what. Maureen explained that it needed to be done; that it was the only way that I would truly be able to escape. They promised that they would both be with me the entire time. After a few minutes of trying to find any way out of the requirement, I finally agreed; I wasn't left with any choice.

When we reached the police station, Steve did all the talking to begin with. He explained to the officers at the front desk that they wished to file a claim of domestic violence and asked if I could be interviewed by a female officer, with both of them in the room as support. I had always known Steve as a very jovial, laid-back friend of Dad's, who never took anything seriously, but this was a different side of him that I had never seen. He spoke with absolute authority and the officer at the desk agreed to his every request.

We were escorted into a private interview room, I was given a glass of water and told that everything said in the room was in complete confidence unless I wished to file a formal complaint. I was assured that I could speak freely about what had happened and no action would be taken unless I agreed to it. With that reassurance, and the comforting death-grip I had on Maureen's hand under the table, I started to recount some of the things that I had experienced over the past two and a half years living with Mr. X.

The officer diligently took notes, and only interrupted occasionally to ask a clarifying question. After about 15-20 minutes, she asked me for Mr. X's full name. I hesitated. This was the question I had dreaded the most. Mr. X had always gone ballistic if I ever told anyone his name. He would always say that a name was a powerful thing and that it was his right and his alone as to whether he chose to divulge it to anyone. The consequences for doing so had always been swift and severe. With both Steve and Maureen reassuring me that I was safe and that it was OK, I finally whispered his name just loud enough for the officer to hear.

She typed the name into the computer on the desk and I saw her eyes skim over the words that it returned to her. Her demeanour changed slightly, and she quietly excused herself, saying that she needed to consult a colleague. A few minutes later she returned with another officer, a man and clearly of higher rank who carried a rather large file with him. He sat down and in a gentle voice expressed his apologies for intruding in on the interview knowing that we had specifically requested to speak to a female officer. He went on to explain that the reason for the intrusion was that Mr. X was indeed known to the police and that the situation was far more serious.

He proceeded to show me the contents of the file that he had brought into the room with him. It was full of details that I just could not comprehend. It had a photo of Mr. X at the front, and several aliases listed underneath, one of which being the name that I had given to the officer moments before. But it wasn't his real name! I continued to read... outstanding warrants in three separate provinces for multiple counts of theft, fraud, and assault. I finally noticed the red flag at the top of the report: "Consider armed and dangerous. Approach with caution".

I couldn't believe what I was seeing, what I was reading. The man that I had been living with for nearly three years was a total stranger. Everything that he had told me about himself and his past was a complete lie!

I have no recollection of the rest of the interview. At some point I must have agreed to make the statement official, because I have a written copy of it. I honestly have no memory of the interview ending, or the drive to Steve and Maureen's house. The next thing I remember is being in the car with Steve the next day, sat outside the house where I lived with Mr. X, watching three other police cruisers turn up and armed police break in through the front door. I remember being absolutely terrified and wanting to run anywhere other than where I was at that very minute. It was at that point that Steve turned to me and said, "Did you know that I am a level 3 black belt in karate?" For some reason, the statement shocked me and brought me to my senses a little bit. He went on to say that with any luck, Mr. X wouldn't be here, but if he was, both himself and the highly trained officers with us would not allow any harm to come to me. I started to relax... a little.

A few moments later, one of the officers emerged from the house and came to escort me inside. He told me that they had searched the house and that it was empty. Because they did not know when Mr. X would return, they could only give me a maximum of 20 minutes to collect a few belongings, including my cat as well as my UK and Canadian passports. The thought that he could return at any moment and I could find myself in the middle of a full-scale armed confrontation cleared my mind totally and I methodically went from room to room collecting only what I needed. My cat, Montey, proved difficult to convince that everything was OK and to get him into his crate, but he eventually complied, albeit with lots of yowling and scratching. I could however only find one passport; my UK passport was nowhere to be found and I eventually concluded that Mr. X had taken it in some strange hope that it would prevent me from leaving the country permanently. When the officer who had escorted me into the house came looking for me, I was ready to go, and we all left without incident.

As anticlimactic as it was, that was it. Four days later I was on a plane bound for Heathrow to start a new life in the UK. I remember as the plane pulled back from the terminal, a single tear rolled down my cheek at the thought of everything that I was leaving behind. Not so much from the past three years, but the life that I had lived before Mr. X. All my friends from Sanctuary, Greg, Steve and Maureen. I wondered if I would ever see them again, or once again ever walk the streets of my beloved Toronto. At the time I doubted that I would ever return, but I resolved that I would not waste this opportunity. I had a chance at a fresh start. No matter what it was going to take, I was going to put whatever I could salvage of my old self back together and move on with my life. Mr. X might have stolen nearly three years of my life, but he was not going to have one second more of it.

***

This move back to the UK was also the catalyst for kicking my marijuana addiction. Several things culminated in a perfect storm of circumstance that provided the environment that I needed to get clean. I was moving to a country where I didn't know anyone other than immediate family. This meant I didn't have the first clue about where to go or who to talk to in order to get access to drugs. Also, at the time of my relocation, the legal position in the UK of possession of marijuana was far more strictly enforced than it was in Canada. This compounded the risk of actively seeking out new contacts in the drug scene – a risk that I was not willing to take. Finally, and most importantly, I had far too much respect and appreciation for what my parents had done to even contemplate bringing drugs into their house. The thought never even crossed my mind.

So, despite the years of dependence, because I was so suddenly thrust into a brand new environment where all of the triggers that fuelled my addiction previously were removed, I had no actual desire or need to smoke a joint. I discovered that my addiction had not been habitual or even substance dependency; it had been escapism, pure and simple. I no longer had anything that I needed to escape from. I was safe, and loved, and whole.

"We must never forget that we may also find meaning in life even when confronted with a hopeless situation, when facing a fate that cannot be changed. For what then matters is to bear witness to the uniquely human potential at its best, which is to transform a personal tragedy into a triumph, to turn one's predicament into a human achievement."

– *Viktor E. Frankl; Austrian psychologist*
& holocaust survivor

Lesson Learned

After reading a story like that, you could easily be forgiven for assuming that the lesson I learned from that situation was not to trust anyone again, but that is not the case. I have learned how to trust people again, though it did take some time and now people do need to earn my trust. But once earned, my trust runs deep.

No, the lesson that I learned from that day in August 2003 is that sometimes it takes a catastrophic event to snap you out of a hopeless situation.

We all end up in bad situations at some point in our lives. Some are the result of our own mistakes or poor judgement. Some may be at the hands of another person with influence over us. Some are just unfortunate happenstance of the stars aligning against us instead of in our favour.

Quite often we think if we just ride it out, things will get better. That if we just knuckle down and put in a bit of extra effort, work a little longer, try a little harder, dig just a little deeper, that things will go back to the way they were or improve the way we would like them to. And most of the time they do.

But there are times when things just won't get any better. Situations where no amount of hard work, dedication, perseverance or belief will change the status quo. If we're not careful we can end up trapped; imprisoned by our belief that things will get better if we just hang on in there a little longer. In those situations, the only way out is for something earth-shattering to happen that forces change.

This becomes more and more true the longer you remain stuck in a situation. The more you fear change, the more you are willing to put up with your circumstances, no matter how much you might hate them – because they are known. There is a reason why the saying "Better the devil you know" exists. It takes monumental change completely beyond your control to force you onto a new path.

Looking back, I honestly believe that if I had told the truth to the doctors at CAMH Mental Hospital after my brush with suicide, that it wouldn't have been enough. Sure, it might have taken me out of the situation with Mr. X temporarily, but I don't think it would have been enough to keep me away. I think that all it would have taken was for me to run into him again on the street (or, more likely, for him to track me down) and for him to turn on the charm again for me to get sucked back in. It took the catastrophic shock of learning the truth in the way that I did to completely break his hold on me.

The problem is that most of the time we only focus on the catastrophic event: the pain, the upheaval and the chaos that it creates. We only see the abyss of the unknown that it throws us into, and we don't see the potential the change can bring. The lesson is to learn that the brightest sunshine comes after the darkest storm. Such catastrophic events can lead to profound change for the better, but only if you embrace them and make the most of the upheaval.

It is scary, yes. It is human nature to fear the unknown. I was terrified sitting on that plane flying to a country I did not remember, not knowing what I was going to do when I landed. But I swore to myself that no matter what happened, I was going to make the most of the second chance I had been given.

Change is nothing to fear; it's a natural part of evolution. You just need to find the strength to go along with it and take what comes. The pain, upheaval and chaos are only temporary. Focus on the opportunity that lies on the other side of change.

This also ties into my revelations about drug addiction and recovery. I full appreciate that my personal experience with beating drug addiction is incredibly mild compared to most cases. However, there is a common thread that I believe every addict can learn from, and that is circumstances and environment.

By changing my circumstances and altering my environment, my reason for taking marijuana disappeared. Thankfully, that was all that was needed in my case because my addiction had not reached the level of substance dependence, of my body physically needing it. I'm not blind to the fact that most addictions come with a level of physical dependence where the process of quitting involves very real and unpleasant physical side effects. More often than not, it's the desire to make the side effects stop that forces most addicts to use again. But removing the underlying cause/need as to why your addiction started in the first place is going to increase your willpower to fight through those withdrawal symptoms that much more. It's the reason why rehab centres are so effective in helping addicts get clean and sober.

So, if you are struggling to kick an addiction on your own, seek help, and don't be afraid to commit yourself to a rehab centre or some other form of self-enforced sobriety. Remove the root cause, the temptation, and the access; then all you are left to fight with is the addiction itself.

"Some changes look negative on the surface but you will soon realize that space is being created in your life for something new to emerge."

– Eckhart Tolle; spiritual teacher

TEN:

Armcos & arm-twisting

Not all the lessons I've learned in my life have come out of dark times, nor has my life been all doom and gloom.

Fast forward to September 2007. I had settled into a great life in the UK. It took a few years, but I had emotionally put myself back together, had a stable job, and had met the man of my dreams – my future husband Nathan.

At the time I was working as a Marketing & Design Manager at Armour Automotive, a car audio manufacturer and distributor, and Nathan worked in the R&D department. I wanted to learn as much about the products that I was going to be marketing as possible, so that winter I volunteered to help Nathan build the demo car that we would take to car shows the following season; a Mazda RX-8 that we affectionately nicknamed 'Rex'.

I had never believed in love at first sight, but that's exactly what it was like with Nathan. Despite the fact that I was dating someone else at the time, I just knew that he was special, and I just had to be with him. We had many common interests; he made me laugh, he was really caring and genuine, and was a great teacher. I found excuses to spend as much time in the R&D workshop as possible, and by the time the 2008 car show season started in March, we couldn't hide our secret relationship any longer and 'officially' starting dating in April.

One of the primary common interests that Nath and I shared was a passion for cars, and unlike many normal couples, we decided that our first holiday away together wasn't going to be a romantic beach getaway to somewhere in the Mediterranean. No, instead we opted to drive to the Nurburgring in German for a three-day track weekend at the notorious Nordschleife racetrack.

If you are not familiar with the Nurburgring Nordschleife circuit, it is one of the most dangerous racetracks in the world. It is 13 miles long with 73 corners, many of which are blind and off-camber. Sir Jackie Stewart nicknamed it 'The Green Hell' and for good reason, as this track claims several lives each year. Once host to the Formula One German Grand Prix; the Nordschleife is now classed as an open toll road as opposed to a dedicated racing circuit, although professional and amateur race events are still held there every year. This means that any car/van/bus/bike/moped/you name it can be on the track at any one time. Add to that the fact that it is your responsibility to stay out of the way of faster vehicles coming up behind you just compounds the challenge of driving this track even more... and we were going there for FUN!?!?!

The drive from Portsmouth (where I was living at the time) to the Nurburgring took about 8 hours on the Friday, and we had an absolute blast. Sharing the driving of Nathan's slightly modified Nissan 200SX S14, playing typical petrol-head car games, and talking about anything and everything. We checked into our B&B, buried deep within the Arden forest a few miles from the track and set out to the circuit early on the Saturday morning.

There is a special feeling about the Nurburgring that is unique to this one track. There is a sense of camaraderie in the paddock and the car parks that I have rarely felt anywhere else. As a petrol-head, it is heaven walking around taking a look at all the amazing cars and chatting to the drivers that make the pilgrimage to this Mecca of racing, to pit themselves and their machines against this challenging circuit. After an hour or so of drooling over supercars, modified sleepers (cars that look unremarkable on the outside, but are in fact highly tuned), and everything in between, we picked up our pre-paid track card and headed out on track for a couple of laps, with Nathan driving. I did my best to pay attention to where Nath was positioning the car at various points during the lap, but with a track this long and with this many corners, everything started to blur together. They say it takes 30-50 laps to learn the layout of this circuit, let alone master it, but we didn't have that sort of time. Before I knew it, it was my turn behind the wheel.

Almost as soon as I got into the lap, I started getting flustered, trying to keep one eye out for faster cars coming up behind and the other eye on where I was actually going. Coming down the hill at Kottenborn, multitasking trying to look in two different directions at once just got too much for me. I completely missed a turning point and nearly ran into the Armco barrier at Aremberg corner. If it hadn't been for Nath's sudden shout "TURN!!!", things would have turned out very differently, and we weren't even a quarter of the way into the lap.

I managed to make it back to the paddock without further incident, but I got out of the car white as a sheet and shaking like a leaf. I turned to Nathan and said that I didn't want to do any more of the laps that we had bought; I was happy to just be a passenger and enjoy the ride. I was totally convinced that if I took the car out one more time, we would not have a car to drive back home in.

The rest of the weekend passed without incident. I thoroughly enjoyed the ride, as I watched Nath get faster and faster with each lap, not to mention being on track with so many other amazing cars. We even managed to share the track with three at-the-time unreleased Nissan GTRs in camouflage livery that were at the Nurburgring undergoing secret testing.

We were scheduled to drive back home on the Monday, but as we had a couple of laps left on our track card, we spent the morning at the track before starting the drive back to the UK. I vividly remember that morning... it was much quieter, as the majority of people had gone back to their daily routines. There was a light mist clearing over the mountains and everything just looked so peaceful – just like on the circuit postcards adorning the shelves of the gift shop.

As we were putting on our helmets before going out for our final lap, Nath crossed his arms on the roof of the car and said to me, "I think you should take this last lap. If you leave having never given it another go, I think you will regret it". My immediate reaction was "Hell no!", but Nath was insistent. He kept reassuring me that it was going to be OK and that I wasn't going to crash the car. The track was quieter, I didn't need to drive fast, it was a beautiful day – he gave me every reason he could think of to convince me to give it one more try. After several minutes of coercing and cajoling, I finally gave up and agreed to do one more lap.

I vividly remember getting back in the car. I was so nervous that I nearly stalled it pulling out of the paddock. I started off slowly, driving almost like I was out on the public road instead of a racetrack, but as the lap progressed, my confidence started to come back. The fact that it was a Monday morning and there were very few other cars on the track meant I was able to just concentrate on my driving and not have to worry about constantly looking behind me as well as where I was going.

Once I passed Aremberg corner without incident, the scene of my previous brush with the Armco barrier, I started to relax and settle into a rhythm. All the things I had read about competitive driving start to come back to me: brake in a straight line before the corner and then ease on the throttle on the way out, look ahead to spot braking points and apexes, and use the full width of the track to flatten out corners.

By the halfway point I was thoroughly enjoying myself, but I opted not to push my luck and so took the flatter outside line around the famous Carraciola-Karussell corkscrew corner. Throughout the final twisty forest section, I had a grin from ear to ear and by the end of the lap I was doing 150mph down the back straight feeling more alive than I ever had before in my life.

"The greatest mistake you can make in life is continually fearing that you will make one."

– Elbert Hubbard; American writer and philosopher

Lesson Learned

The lesson that I learned from that final 15-minute lap of the Nurburgring is that you are capable of amazing things if you just have the courage to get back in the car!

Anything in life that is worthwhile is never easy. You are going to make mistakes, you are going to get it wrong every now and then, and you might even crash. That is part of life, that is the process of learning where your limits are and figuring out what you need to develop and learn in order to reach beyond those limits. But if you live in fear of the barrier, just like I did that morning before deciding to get back behind the wheel, you will never progress.

Don't let a fear of failure hold you back from experiencing everything that this life has to offer. Don't reach your twilight years and think, "I wish I had…". You should aim to look back on your life and marvel at the things you have done, the experiences you have had, and the successes you have enjoyed.

Many people say that failure is a sign that something was not meant to be. Well I, and many successful people, would disagree with that statement. Consider these famous "failures":

) Michael Jordon was dropped from his high school basketball team for "lack of skill"

) The Beatles were rejected by Decca Records, who said "They have no future in show business"

) Abraham Lincoln failed in business three times and went through seven failed campaigns before becoming President of the United States

) Albert Einstein was not able to speak until the age of four. He was expelled from school and his teachers described him as "mentally slow".

) Steve Jobs was forced out of Apple, the company he co-founded, at the age of 30.

) Thomas Edison's teachers told him he was "too stupid to learn anything"

) Bill Gates dropped out of Harvard University and his first company, Traf-O-Data was an epic failure

⟩ Oprah Winfrey was fired from her job as a news reporter because she was "unfit for TV"

⟩ Marilyn Monroe was dropped by 20th Century Fox after 1 year because she wasn't "pretty or talented enough to be an actress"

⟩ Henry Ford had three failed businesses before he founded Ford Motor Company

⟩ Stephen King's first book, *Carrie*, was rejected 30 times

⟩ Soichiro Honda was passed over for an engineering job at Toyota and left unemployed

⟩ J.K. Rowling was unemployed, divorced and raising her daughter on social security whilst writing the first *Harry Potter* novel, which was rejected 12 times before being signed up by a publisher.

Fear is a natural emotion; it is ingrained in us as humans beings as a safety mechanism to ensure the survival of the species, and shouldn't be ignored. However, it shouldn't be used as an excuse to never try anything new, challenging or even a little scary either. Instead, turn that fear into adrenaline. Use it as a warning that what you are about to do is potentially dangerous or risky and needs you to be on top form. But with that focus and determination, go for it with everything you've got.

I have used this lesson numerous times since that road trip. I've started my own business, I got married, I've been skydiving, written my first, and now this second, book... All these things were only possible because I had the courage to get back in the car. In fact, I use the mantra "Just get back in the car" whenever I am faced with something that scares me but that I know I should or need to do.

On our way out of the Nurburgring gates that Monday, Nathan pulled the car over and disappeared momentarily into the gift shop, saying that he would be back in a minute. When he returned, he carried two carbon fibre rings that he had bought, one for him and one for me. He intended them to just be a reminder of the great weekend that we had had, but mine has been a symbol of strength and determination that adorns my finger next to my wedding ring to this very day. If you can, find a symbol of what can be possible if you simply choose to believe. It may be a religious symbol; a depiction of your potential future beyond the fear; or a memory of a fear conquered. Whatever it is, carry it with you always and use it to find the determination to live everything that life has to offer.

"Let the night come,
before the fight's won
Some might run against the test.
But those that triumph,
embrace the fight 'cause
Their fear then proves
that courage exists."

– *"Can't Hold Us" by Macklemore & Ryan Lewis ft. Ray Dalton (**The Heist**, 2012; Macklemore LLC)*

ELEVEN:

"Do you have a minute!"

My new life in the UK wasn't all sunshine and roses... fast forward three years to the winter of 2009. My parents had decided to move back to Canada, because Mum found it too difficult to reconcile the UK that she knew when they were first married and the UK that they had moved back to in 2001. My relationship with Nathan had also hit a bit of a temporary brick wall and I had moved out to live on my own in a small one-bed flat about 10 minutes from work. Money was tight but I was just about making ends meet. Then the economic crash happened. Wages were frozen, the price of fuel and utilities started to rise, and things became just that little bit harder.

I was still working for the same company where I had met Nathan. Though there had been some restructuring of the business around me, no one was being let go, so I felt fairly secure in my position. Secure enough at least to have a quiet chat with my boss to explain my financial situation and to ask if there was any possibility of a pay rise, even if just a meagre one.

What I would later learn was that the recession had started to take its toll on the company and redundancy talks were already taking place behind closed doors. To my boss's credit, he didn't laugh in my face at my request. Instead he said that he understood the situation that I was facing, and would see what he could do.

A few weeks later, on December 1st, my boss called me into a meeting in the boardroom. I immediately knew something was not right when I was asked to close the door but was in no way prepared for what was to happen next. My boss started to quietly explain the economic situation the company found itself in: share prices had plummeted, the cost of shipping goods in from China had skyrocketed, and all of that combined with a general unease from consumers unwilling to spend money had led to the decision that the company needed to tighten its belt... starting with the marketing department. The marketing budget was to be cut in half, effective immediately, and consumer shows were being cut from the campaign completely.

I sat and listened, blindly unaware of what all this preamble was leading up to. In my business naivety, I expected this conversation to turn to ways in which the department could reduce costs whilst still maintaining a presence to the buying public. Little did I know that the budget-cutting measures that had already been discussed involved far more than just departmental spending.

It was starting to become obvious that he couldn't dance around the subject any longer, and so my boss just came out and gave me the news he had been building up to: my position of Design & Marketing Manager was being made redundant, and only a junior graphic design position was being kept in the company to fulfil the need for packaging artwork and sales literature. I was to consider myself on notice.

Needless to say, I was stunned! I could not believe what I was hearing and was convinced this had to be either a horrible dream or a terrible mistake. After a moment or two, when I just sat in shocked silence, my boss continued to inform me that I was expected to work my notice period until the Christmas break and that my employment would officially terminate on January 1st. I was told that I could take the rest of the day off to adjust to the news but was expected to be back at work the next day. I was also asked not to discuss what had been said until management had had a chance to inform the rest of my team... after I had left.

Unsurprisingly, the rest of that day is a bit of a blur. I remember walking back to my desk and telling my two team members that they were wanted in the boardroom. One of them asked if I was OK, to which I replied no but didn't have time to talk about it. I don't remember the drive home or the long walk up the flight of stairs to my flat. I do remember standing in my living room and the sudden gravity of what had just happened hitting me like a ton of bricks and breaking down into uncontrollable crying.

I vaguely remember Mike, another director and my old boss who had originally hired me, giving me a call at some point to apologise for not giving me a heads-up of what was coming. He apparently had known for a couple of weeks, but obviously wasn't allowed to say anything. Nathan stopped by the flat that afternoon after work to make sure I was OK, which of course I wasn't, but I tried to put on a brave face as best I could. I can't remember whether I ate anything that evening, and I doubt I got any sleep that night thinking about how I was going to face walking back into that office the following morning.

The following three weeks in the lead-up to Christmas were the worst that I can remember. Having to go to work every day like nothing had happened was emotionally exhausting. Day after day handing over projects and work to the junior designer who was going to replace me, who I had hired straight out of college, felt like a knife in the back. And the constant questions of "How are you?", "What are you going to do after this?" and "Are you going to be OK?", started to really grate on my nerves and I couldn't wait for it to all be over.

Before I knew it, that final day came and went. No fuss, no ceremony, not even much of a thank you. I think I got a card that people had passed around to sign, but that was it. Five years of loyalty and dedication, over in what felt like a heartbeat. I didn't have much time to think or reflect on what I was going to do next, as I was scheduled to fly out to Canada to spend Christmas with my parents the very next day.

The following morning, I got in a cab to the airport and seven hours later was back in Toronto – the first time I had been back since that fateful day in 2003.

What very few people knew was that for the previous nine months I had secretly been looking for a new job. Though I had felt secure in my job at Armour, I wasn't overly happy there. The company culture wasn't great and there was a widely-held notion that management didn't really care about the common workers – a sentiment that had been doubly reinforced in my mind by recent events. But the recession was in full effect, and one of the unwritten rules of business economics is that in tough times marketing budgets are always the first to be cut, so no one was hiring designers or marketeers. Even doubling my job-hunting efforts after receiving the news about my redundancy had no effect, and any potential prospects of new employment were thin to non-existent.

So, by the time I arrived in Toronto for Christmas, I had no idea what I was going to do. Real panic was starting to set in, but I was convinced that I didn't want to give up and move back in with Mum and Dad. Not only did I feel I was too old to continue to rely on my parents to bail me out of bad situations, but I was not mentally prepared to come back to Toronto for any more than a two-week visit – my fear of running into Mr. X again was all too real.

The answer to my problem came out of a very innocent conversation during a visit with family friends Steve and Maureen, who had taken me in when I escaped Mr. X. Like many discussions during that week, the conversation turned to what I was going to do when I returned home. I explained about the lack of jobs in my profession at present and that I really didn't know what I was going to do. And then, with one brief statement, Steve was about to change everything...

"If no one is going to hire you to do what you want to do, and you don't want to do anything else – you should do it for yourself."

He went on to explain that he had been in an almost identical situation to me a year or so before. That he had lost his job only to find that no one was hiring full-time staff to do that job. However, just because no one was hiring staff to do that job didn't mean that job didn't need doing. Companies would rather pay a consultant a one-off fee to do the work as opposed to the ongoing expense of hiring a full-time member of staff. He now worked as a self-employed consultant, earning far more than he did before as an employee and with the freedom to work his own hours.

I was fascinated! I had always thought that it would be cool to run my own design agency, and here was someone I knew, trusted and respected explaining that it was completely possible to do it right now! I spent the rest of that evening picking Steve's brains on everything he did when he set up on his own. There were obviously going to be some differences, given the fact that we were involved in different industries and that I was going to be setting up my company in the UK and not Canada, but I absorbed all the advice I could.

I finally had my answer and was able to enjoy Christmas surrounded by family and filled with a sense of excitement for the first time in years. This was the start of something new! I flew back home January 2nd, and January 3rd, I logged onto the Companies House website and registered SWATT Design as a sole-trading business.

To this day I remember the feeling of sitting at my computer that first working day of 2010 and thinking, I am now the master of my own destiny. It's now down to me whether I succeed or fail. I have four months of redundancy money to live on, so this needs to work by then – no ifs, ands, or buts. Let's do this!

"You can't outwit fate by standing on the sidelines placing little side bets about the outcome of life... if you don't play you can't win."

– Judith McNaught; American novelist and 1st female executive producer at CBS Radio

Lesson Learned

The lesson I learned from those two vastly different, but very life-changing, conversations is that sometimes you need to make your own opportunities.

Life is never meant to be easy – if it were, we would all be winning at it. There are always going to be trials and tribulations; periods of your life where it feels like every door of opportunity is being slammed in your face. Most people, when faced with that sort of situation, will accept it as just being the way it has to be at that moment, but it doesn't have to be.

Every situation, good or bad, presents us with a choice. Sometimes that choice is not always clear, and sometimes that choice can be as limited as choosing HOW to accept the situation as just being the way it has to be at that moment (graciously or grudgingly) – but there is ALWAYS a choice. When faced with redundancy and no prospects of new employment, my choice was to give up and move back home or create my own opportunity by starting my own business. I choose to take the opportunity that presented itself. After all, who knew when I would ever get the chance again?

Sure, it was exciting, but make no mistake, it was one of the scariest choices I've ever made. I was opting for the route with no safety net if things went wrong. Of course, it was hard work that involved a massive learning curve and provided little margin for error. And yes, I made some monumental mistakes (some of which you'll read about in coming chapters), but for the first time in my life I was truly the master of my own destiny. My success or failure was completely in my own hands, and I had to make it work.

As I've mentioned before, Dad had a saying when I was growing up: "Prepare for the worse, hope the best; that way you are ready for anything." That piece of advice helped me get through the first few years of running my business. From trying to anticipate what could go wrong and planning for how to deal with it if it did happen, through to being optimistic about every opportunity and having the courage to take hold of the best ones and run with them. And it worked...

Ten years later, my business is still going strong. It's taken a few very different turns than what I originally imagined, but I am proud of what I have built up over the years and don't begrudge the sometimes painful lessons learned along the way. Fate it would seem has an interesting sense of humour, as not two months before writing this very chapter, Nathan was made redundant from the same company where I had been ten years earlier. When faced with the same choice, he also opted to take the opportunity that presented itself of creating his own destiny and has joined me as a partner in my new business, SWATT Books.

So, I encourage you to look carefully at the choices that present themselves during the inevitable turning points in your life. Think about what opportunities, no matter how scary, are made possible by what on the face of it could feel like a hopeless situation. Find the courage to grab those opportunities with both hands and recognise the destiny you can forge for yourself. I can, hand-on-heart, say that the decision to start my own business at the peak of the worst recession in recent memory was one of the best decisions that I have ever made – even though it was far from being the easiest or safest road to travel.

The journey I have taken these past 10 years to becoming a successful entrepreneur has changed me significantly – probably more so than all the other experiences in this book so far. It has given me the opportunity to learn fully who I am. Many of the lessons that I have illustrated in these pages (even those stemming from more personal events unrelated to my business) have been revealed as a result of my business journey. Despite all the trials and tribulations that I have faced starting my business (and there have been many) I would not willingly trade the experience to go back to a 'normal' job. In all honesty, I don't think I'm 'employable' anymore, having been my own boss for so long.

Sure, it has been scary, uncertain and unpredictable. There have been countless sleepless nights, stresses, setbacks and extremely difficult decisions along the way, but if you are given the opportunity to start your own business, doing something that you are passionate about – DO IT!!! Take the lessons from Chapters 5 and 10 about not letting opportunities slip through your fingers and have the courage to "Just get back in the car" to see what exciting reality lies on the other side of the fear of failure. By all means, have a contingency plan in the back of your mind, but put everything you have into your Plan A and go for it. You will never know what is possible until you try.

———————————

"The reason a lot of people do not recognise opportunity is because it usually goes around wearing overalls looking like hard work."

———————————

– Thomas A. Edison; American inventor and businessman

TWELVE:

The international incident

The first few months of running SWATT Design were tough to say the least. There's no real blueprint, no simple step-by-step guide on how to start and run a successful business, because every business is different. Even taking an MBA won't give you all the answers, so the learning curve I experienced in that first six months felt more like a vertical climb up the North Face of Everest.

Sure, I knew graphic design inside and out. I knew that when a job came in, that I could handle anything it threw at me, but I had no idea HOW to get a job in! I had never really worked in a public design agency before – the majority of my working experience had been for in-house design departments in private companies. Questions such as, "Where do you find clients?", "How do you approach those clients?", "What do you include in a pitch?", even ones as simple as "How much should I charge?" were all completely unknown quantities to me.

Then there was the business of actually running a BUSINESS: bookkeeping, client management, marketing, budgets, invoicing, insurance, infrastructure, tax, and a million and one other things that I had no idea about. I felt massively in over my head.

My saving grace in those first six months, believe it or not, was HMRC, Her Majesty's Revenue & Customs... yup, the government. Everyone thinks that the government is quick to penalise companies and individuals when things go wrong, and to an extent they are, but they don't WANT businesses to fail. They have a treasure-trove of information available to new business owners to help you through every facet of starting a business in the UK. At the time that I started SWATT Design, they even ran free half-day workshops on topics that were required for legal compliance, such as tax, bookkeeping and import/ export. Unfortunately, due to budget cuts I don't think these workshops are running any more, but it's worth looking into.

Once I had the basics down, it was onto finding people to support me. Queue my introduction to business networking. I hated networking with a passion in the beginning, mainly because I lacked all confidence in myself and my business. The idea of standing up in a room-full of strangers and talking about myself and my business was tantamount to torture in my mind. However, the odd once or twice that I forced myself to go, I was introduced to people who were able to answer many of the questions that I had, and reassure me that I was indeed on the right track.

Unfortunately, none of this was able to solve the most immediate and important problem that I was facing... that we were still in the middle of the worst global recession in modern memory prior to the COVID-19 pandeamic. This meant that finding clients in the UK willing to spend money on design and marketing at that time was nigh on impossible. After much research and plenty of trial and error, the answer to that little dilemma turned out to be the internet and the wonderful shark tank that is online bidding sites. These are websites where companies and individuals can post tasks they need doing, for service providers to submit a bid. 99% of the time, contracts are awarded to the lowest bidder; usually to contractors from low-income countries such as India or China who can easily afford to undercut Western freelancers. However, there were the odd unicorn clients hiding in these sites who were willing to pay for experience. Finding these rarities became my mission; every morning I would spend at least 1-2 hours trawling through the various bidding sites, bidding on anything and everything that I was capable of doing, knowing that out of every 30-40 bids that were rejected for being too high, there was going to be one who was willing to pay for my experience and expertise.

That was how I survived the recession, working remotely via the wonders of technology with companies in regions not yet affected by the global economic downturn such as Australia and the Middle East. But my naivety and severe lack of business acumen was about to bite me on the ass – and the bank account.

To do business on any of these bidding sites, you need to comply with certain regulations, and so there was a contract put in place for every job that was tendered. In my innocence, I assumed this meant that I was protected. Little did I realise that these contracts were massively skewed in the clients' favour, and from a 'legal' standpoint, as a contractor, these were as leaky as a broken sieve. A lesson I learned in spectacular fashion when I landed my first "big" contract.

I won a bid to produce a 300+ page catalogue for a medical supply company in Australia which specialised in geriatric and elderly care products for nursing homes. All in, this contract was going to be worth nearly £3,000 for around three months' work. I eagerly got to work, and was in regular communications with the client, reviewing proofs and discussing direction and amendments. I thought everything was going well but more and more changes kept coming through, even to sections that had already been approved. Work kept dragging on and on; three months turned into four and then into five. I asked the client if they would be willing to release some of the fee (which was being held in escrow by the bidding site) to cover expenses due to the project going past its original timeframe, but they refused. Then all communication stopped. I didn't hear anything for over a week. When you consider that I was previously in contact with the client multiple times a day, the silence was deafening.

After numerous attempts to get in touch with them failed, I contacted the management of the bidding site. I explained that the project was pretty much finished as far as I was concerned; all pages were designed, and we were just going through proofing at the time that communication stopped. Their reply was that it was more than likely that something had come up with the client that had distracted their attention away from the project. This was something they claimed was common. They advised me that I could file a claim on the site which would be sent to the client from them as opposed to from me, and that this usually prompted a response. Dutifully I did as I was told and filed a claim. Two days later the client cancelled the contract, stating the reason being that the work provided by the supplier (me) had not been what was requested.

That was it. Contract terminated. Escrow refunded to the client and I received nothing! Five months work, no payment, AND they walked away with the PDF proofs of the entire catalogue that I had produced. I couldn't believe it!

I went back to the management of the bidding site and was promptly told that they were fully within their rights to cancel the project on the grounds they provided. My argument that they had indeed received the completed catalogue fell on deaf ears. I then contacted a contracts lawyer and it was then that I discovered just how woefully exposed I had been.

During the free consultation with the lawyer, he pointed out how the bidding site contract did indeed offer me next to no protection as a service provider; and that it was my responsibility to have provided my own contract for the client to sign before commencing the work. Just to rub salt in the wound, he went on to explain that I had in no way protected the PDF proofs that I had sent to the client from being used without my permission or payment. If I wanted to fight it, I "might" have a case, but it would mean fighting it in the Australian judicial system, meaning I would need to fly to Australia for any and all hearings, all at my expense. As a final twist of the knife, he added that I wouldn't be able to claim for my travelling expenses if the ruling should happen to go in my favour.

So, I had no choice but to let it go and chalk up those five months as a massive rookie mistake. Given that I was in serious need of some income for my fledgling business, "rookie mistake" was an understatement!

"Mistakes are a part of being human. Appreciate your mistakes for what they are: precious life lessons that can only be learned the hard way."

– Al Franken; American politician

Lesson Learned

Aside from the obvious business lessons that I learned from this experience: the need to put my own contract in place; making sure every client signs it before you undertake a minute's worth of work; and to protect all proofs from being used for anything other than proofing; the overarching lesson I learned from those five months of wasted work was that some lessons need to be learned the hard way.

But let's start with the obvious mistakes first: setting up a watertight contract and protecting your work. Every business, regardless of size, industry or customer base needs to undertake some level of due diligence. To do this effectively, unfortunately you need to switch your mindset to one which expects the worst from people and then come up with ways to protect yourself if you should happen to be proved correct.

The starting point is to set up a simple but effective contract for all work you undertake... before you commence the work! This can be as simple as an email or a letter stating the work that you will do and what the cost will be. It depends on how involved the work is, what your relationship is with the potential client, and the value of the contract. The client agrees in writing and away you go. However, some industries and types of work require a more robust set of terms and conditions to accompany that statement of work... and this is where it can get trickier. I've tried to write my own T&Cs and frankly it's just not worth it. These are intended as a legally binding statement, so you do need to have an understanding of contract law to ensure that what you are requiring of your client is not only reasonable but also legal within your jurisdiction. Seek help and advice if you plan on writing your own T&Cs; or at least pay for a professionally vetted T&Cs template appropriate for your given industry.

As for protecting your work, the premise is the same. Indulge your inner pessimist and think how any unscrupulous client might use your work before they have paid for it. If, like me, you are providing proofs or beta versions for your client to review, make sure that the files are locked in some fashion to prevent someone tampering with them or outright using them before they are authorised to do so. Consider adding a logo or watermark to the file as a visual brand of ownership; or password protect the file from being altered and prevent content from being copied and pasted out of it. All this is fairly straightforward to do when generating PDF files.

This may feel like overkill for some people; especially those who are more trusting or are working with people they know and have already built a relationship with. But trust me, even the most loyal client can turn rogue on you, as you will learn shortly. It's better to be safe than sorry. Every reasonable client will merely see these safeguards as a sign of professionalism, not an indicator that you are doubting their trustworthiness.

Now let's explore the more profound and less obvious lesson that I learned from this experience: learning some lessons the hard way.

During the preceding months of research and learning I had put into starting my business, the topic of contracts had come up multiple times. I knew it was important, but in my naivety assumed that the contract put in place by the bidding site was sufficient. After all, by providing the platform for the contract to take place, they were technically the suppliers for both parties. No one except a contract lawyer would have been able to convince me to the contrary.

It also wasn't the first time that I had heard of the concept of protecting business IP (intellectual property) i.e. my proofs. But again, I thought that by uploading them via the bidding site and not just sending them via an unsecured email was sufficient protection. I needed for things to go terribly wrong for me to learn the full extent of what is meant by "protecting business IP".

We all have similar blind spots. Whether it be in business or in our personal lives, there are things that deep down you know, things that any number of people can warn you about, but that just don't really hit home until the worst-case scenario happens. It's human nature to believe our own narrative over that of others, unless we attribute a certain level of higher credibility to that other person; for example that other person being a specialist in contract law.

So, whether we like it or not, there are some lessons that can only be learned through bitter experience. It's "learning the hard way", as the saying goes. The key is learning the lesson the first time round, and not making the same mistake twice.

It can also be easy for the more stubborn of us to dig our heels in and insist that we know best – especially if the lesson involves a very personal subject that touches a nerve. It is imperative in those situations to at least listen to others, if not take their advice. If enough people are advising against something, then you need to take your ego out of the equation long enough to at least step back for a second and look at the situation dispassionately; to see if you are really making the right call.

Needless to say, I did indeed learn my lesson, and organised drawing up a contract which included a robust set of terms and conditions. I also put in place processes to protect my work. Did all this protect me from never being taken advantage of again? No, but it certainly protected me from not receiving anything in return for work completed and from having proofs essentially being stolen.

No business or person is ever going to be 100% protected from things going wrong. Bad things do and always will happen in some form or another. All we can do is protect ourselves as best as possible, and learn from every bump in the road so as to avoid hitting the same pothole further down the line.

"We all learn lessons in life. Some stick, some don't. I have always learned more from rejection and failure than from acceptance and success."

– Henry Rollins; musician, singer & songwriter

THIRTEEN:

A knife in the back

By 2012, I had started to get my head wrapped around how to run, and live off, my own business. I had a steady stream of clients and was able to earn enough to cover my bills, which thankfully were a lot more manageable since Nathan and I had reconciled our differences and moved into a house in Eastleigh together. I felt like I was starting to finally make some progress.

I was still relying heavily on bidding sites for most of my initial new client generation. But once I had won a bid and successfully completed a project, I was usually able to keep a relationship going with the client so that they would come directly to me for new work instead of posting it for open tender.

Not all jobs posted on these bidding sites were stand-alone projects. There were the occasional ongoing freelance positions posted by companies looking for remote or part-time team members. These are always highly-coveted job postings with plenty of competition, as they represent more secure long-term contracts with regular steady income. One such company that piqued my interest was a print brokerage company, TPH, based in London, who were looking for a design consultant to manage pre-flight work for them before artwork was sent to their contracted print facilities in eastern Europe for production. 'Pre-flight' in the printing industry is the process where artwork is reviewed to ensure it is compliant with the print specifications of the job and doesn't contain any errors that could cause printing problems or quality issues. Due to my extensive background in print design and my understanding of how the print process worked from a technical standpoint, I won the contract quite easily and overnight TPH became my most lucrative client.

TPH primarily handled book printing projects, and this was my introduction to the world of book design and typesetting. On top of running several pre-flight checks a day, 75% of which would require some form of artwork adjustment or correction (which I was able to charge an hourly rate for), TPH started passing me referrals for customers who wanted a book printed but didn't have anyone to produce the artwork for them. Within 6 months of starting to work for TPH, not only were they my highest paying client, they were also my primary source of new business. Business was booming – I started to rent out a studio space in a shared creative working unit and hired my first part-time freelancer. But all was not as it seemed.

Odd little isolated incidents started cropping up here and there. It started with a very sudden change of company name. One day, my contact at TPH rang up to inform me that they were changing their company name, effective immediately. No reference to their previous trading name was to be mentioned anywhere or under any circumstances. It seemed a little strange and when I enquired as to the reason for this sudden change, he simply said it was for legal reasons. Though I was still fairly new to the business management world, I did know that companies changed their trading name on occasion, so thought nothing more of it and dutifully complied with their request to update all of my records and invoices with the new details. For the purposes of this story, I'll continue to refer to them here as TPH.

I then started to receive occasional phone calls from TPH customers, saying that they had not received their printed books and hadn't been able to get any answers out of anyone at head office. Being loyal to my client, I would always defend TPH against any accusations of wrongdoing and assured the customer that I would follow up and get the matter resolved. Most of the time that would be successful, but every now and then my contact at TPH would explain that there was more to the story than the customer had revealed to me and that they would handle it. Despite the slowly increasing frequency and severity of such complaints, and despite my gut screaming that something wasn't quite right, I remained loyal – they were after all my golden goose. That is until payment of my own invoices to TPH started to be paid late.

It started innocuously enough. Payments would be late by a week or two here and there but were usually paid as soon as I sent a reminder. But then a week or two started to become three or four weeks, and one reminder started to become several before payment was received – and even then, not always for the full amount. Then the payments stopped. My contact assured me that it was a temporary cashflow issue that would be resolved soon; I just needed to be patient. By this time, I had been working with TPH for nearly two years, and so I trusted that they would make good on their promises and continued to undertake the work.

Each month-end invoice that I sent would be accompanied by a reminder of previous invoices that were still outstanding. At least once a week I would ring my contact to ask when I would get paid. Things started to get desperate financially and I began making cuts to my own business by drastically axing any unnecessary spending and I was forced to let go of my new freelancer. By the time three months of non-payment had come and gone, I had no choice but to issue TPH with the ultimatum that if they didn't clear all outstanding invoices I would suspend all pre-flight work until payment was received, or take legal action.

A few days after the ultimatum was sent, I received a letter in the post via recorded delivery. The envelope was addressed from the Civil Judiciary of London; inside was a notice that a claim had been filed against me with London Small Claims Court... the claimant was TPH!!!

I was beside myself with shock – I couldn't believe what I was reading. According to the claim, errors that I had made on artwork for a print job six months prior had resulted in the customer demanding a refund for all printing costs, which TPH were demanding that I pay. I clearly remembered the job they were referring to and recalled that, yes, there had been issues with the print, but they were not as a result of any artwork problems. I had even discussed the job at length with my contact and he had assured me that I had done all that I could. Miraculously, the amount of the claim was the exact amount that TPH owed me in unpaid invoices!

As I continued to read the additional information that the court had included with the claim, I discovered that I had a right to defend the case and to lodge a counter claim if I so wished. The catch... it was going to cost me to do so – nearly £500 once all was said and done. I could afford to pay it, but only if I took it out of the money that was earmarked for my salary. After I pulled myself together, I went home early and prepared to tell Nathan the bad news.

Naturally he was furious and kept demanding to know where he could find this company so that he could go and demand they drop this ludicrous lawsuit and pay me what they owed. I eventually calmed him down enough to have a rational conversation and we decided the best course of action was to not only fight the suit but to raise a counter claim for the unpaid invoices – we would find a way of coping with me bringing home a reduced salary for a while if it gave me a shot at finally getting paid the money I was owed.

It's insane the amount of paperwork that is involved in putting a claim through the small claims court system in the UK. Every aspect requires a form to be filled in. All claims need to be backed up with supporting evidence which needs to be submitted with said forms; and all need to be sent to the court AND the other party by recorded delivery so that there is proof it was sent and received. It dragged on for months; all the while my business suffered drastically.

Not only was I distracted, in emotional turmoil over the feelings of utter betrayal and having to siphon off money to pay for legal costs, but my once lucrative (and now only) source of new clients had dried up overnight. I only had my bank of existing contacts and clients to keep me going. Thankfully, that, along with a reinvigorated focus on new client acquisition by any means necessary, meant that I finally made it to the day of the hearing with my business still afloat... but only just.

It is a generally held statute in UK law that small claims court hearings are always held in the jurisdiction of the initial claimant. As TPH was registered as a London-based company, that meant the hearing for our case was to be held at the Royal Courts of Justice at The Old Bailey in London – home of the Supreme Court and seat of ultimate judicial power in the United Kingdom.

Knowing that Nathan would be extremely hard-pressed to keep his emotions under control if faced with the people who had put me through so much stress, anxiety and upset, I opted to go to the hearing on my own, putting on a brave face that I would be fine. The trip to London on the train from Eastleigh felt at once very long and all too short. Nervous and quite apprehensive, I arrived at The Old Bailey nearly a full hour before my hearing.

If you have never been to The Old Bailey in London, it is the most imposing and intimidating building you could ever enter. Just walking through the main doors into the great hall filled me with dread. Its gothic architecture, high placed narrow windows, and granite construction gives it an ominous feeling of a prison. Seeing Supreme Court judges walking around in their scarlet robes and powdered wigs, the very men and women who write and uphold the law of the land, instantly made me feel as if I was guilty.

I eventually found my way through the maze of interconnecting hallways to the courtroom where my hearing was to be held, and waited to be called in. As the minutes ticked by, my already tightly wound nerves got worse and worse. Every new person who would enter the waiting room would make me jump, thinking this was going to be the moment of confrontation. I have always feared confrontation, but since my experiences with Mr. X, those fears had intensified a hundredfold. I dreaded the very thought of being in the same room and coming face to face with my accusers. I knew that if they turned up for the hearing, my chances of winning were next to none, as

I would be so terrified of saying the wrong thing in fear of retaliation that I would be hard-pressed to get any words out at all. I was a wreck.

After what felt like hours, but couldn't have been more than 10 minutes, my name was called, and I was ushered into a small courtroom. The room consisted of two small boardroom tables set side-by-side with a wide gap between, and at the front of the room on a raised platform was the judge's bench, with a royal seal cast in steel mounted to the wall behind. As I took my seat, I looked up and with a visible sigh of relief found that I was alone in the room with the judge; TPH had not sent a representative to the hearing.

The judge could clearly see that I was extremely nervous and visibly shaking. He offered me a glass of water, gave me a moment to calm down and then explained what was going to happen. All I had to do was answer his questions truthfully and to the best of my ability. No one else was going to walk in, so we were just going to have a conversation.

In my fear of not really knowing what to expect from the day and wanting to be prepared for anything, I had clearly over-prepared – something that the judge actually complimented me on as he noted the folder of notes, correspondence and evidence that I took out of my bag. Starting with the original claim against me, the judge read out to me the full claim and 'evidence' that TPH had provided to the count. I felt myself starting to get more and more upset as the full extent of what TPH was accusing me of started to sink in. But it was all lies.

When my turn came to speak, I was easily able to refute all TPH's claims. I provided detailed evidence of conversations with both the customer and TPH where issues were discussed and resolved. I concluded by presenting the judge with a written sign-off from the customer, acknowledging that they were 100% happy with the artwork and approved the book to go to print. When I was finished, the judge sat silent for a moment and then, apparently satisfied with my answers, moved on to my counter claim.

Again, the judge read the full extent of my claim and the response the court had received from TPH as to why they had not paid me; stating their original claim as grounds to withhold payment. He asked me to give him copies of all my invoices, and the mountain of correspondence that I had collated, showing that TPH had told me they were willing to pay and that the original claim was never once mentioned.

The judge took even less time to consider the counter claim, and within moments stated that he was ready to make his ruling. He found no grounds to uphold TPH's original claim against me. Furthermore, the fact that they had not bothered to turn up to the hearing and had wasted the court's time showed an utter disregard, not only for the court, but for me as well. The original claim was thrown out and my counter claim was upheld. The judge then started to ask me for a running total of my court costs, travel expenses to attend the hearing, and amount of statutory interest I was due. Adding the figures to the total of unpaid invoices on a calculator, he then asked me to take a guess at the amount of paid work I had lost out on by being in court instead of working.

This was the one question of the day that I was completely unprepared for! I stammered for a moment, trying to think of an appropriate figure, and settled for the number of hours of work that I had rescheduled in order to take the day off (which wasn't that much, as work was getting thin on the ground). The judge looked at me and smiled, then as if reading my mind, asked me instead how much time I could be working if I wasn't in court today. A bit unsure of myself, I replied that it was double what I had previously offered, and with a wink the judge added the figure to his calculator. He cleared his throat and in a loud and very official voice stated that he was awarding me a County Court Judgement (CCJ) against TPH for the grand total of £5,500. Case closed.

I nearly collapsed with relief – it was finally over!

Or so I thought. Literally the very next day after receiving the court order, TPH declared bankruptcy. I added my name to the list of debtors, but after another year of fighting I never saw a penny of what I was owed. To add insult to injury, I later discovered that the company was back up and running the day after declaring bankruptcy under a new name, new address, and new director... though customers whom I was still in contact with confirmed that nothing in fact was different.

The more research I did to find a way to recuperate anything I could, the more I discovered just how unscrupulous TPH had been. The mysterious name change shortly after I started working with them was the result of a similar CCJ that had been brought against them under their original trading name. In effect, they had been completing just enough jobs to keep a relatively clean reputation online, but had been skimming thousands off the top... every 4 or 5 jobs, they would keep the money paid to them for printing, and not even produce the books. If the customer complained enough, they would get the job printed but then never pay the printer they contracted. It was disgusting, immoral, and I couldn't believe I had not only fallen for it but had defended them when customers had tried to convince me of the truth.

I had been taken advantage of yet again.

***

Though I never received a single penny of the money owned to me, my experience with TPH did have a silver lining in the life of my business – it helped me to discover my true niche.

All the clients that TPH were funnelling my way were authors, and the work that I was doing for them centred around the design, typesetting and preparation of books. I had always loved books and have been an avid reader since childhood. One of my earliest memories is of Mum reading to me at bedtime the short stories from *The World of Christopher Robin* by A.A. Milne. This is a book that still has pride of place on my bookshelf today. Being introduced to these authors and working on their fascinating books gave me the opportunity to combine two of my biggest passions – design and books. I discovered an entire demographic of self-publishing authors who needed and valued my services as a graphic designer, and my skills with typography made me ideally suited to the work.

Not only was the work rewarding but it was also very lucrative, and the independent author community was one where referrals were far more commonplace than in the corporate world that I had been trying to service previously. So, I took the decision to start specialising in book design and typesetting. I started to reduce the general corporate design work that I was doing and focused solely on authors. It wasn't long before one of those book design clients, Paul Blanchard (funnily enough, one of the people that TPH forwarded to me), rang me out of the blue one afternoon to run an "idea" past me. He explained that the books that I had been designing for him were being self-published through a platform called Ingram Spark. He had someone who managed that process for him, but that person was relocating to Australia and wasn't going to be able to continue the work. He asked me if I was willing to take over managing the account and his self-publishing process for him.

To this day I remember standing in my living room being rendered dumbfounded and speechless by the question. I managed to stammer that I was flattered that he thought of me, but that I had no experience in publishing. Paul went on to say, "That's OK, neither did Connor before he took over. And besides, I'll only let you loose on my books before I let you take on on my clients' books."

"Wait... clients' books?" Sure enough, Paul was the founder of a high-profile PR and reputation management agency and he had starting offering white label book publishing services to his clients as a way of boosting their credibility.

My mind started to trip over itself running through the possibilities. There was clearly a market for this – Paul was evidence of that. What would it do to my business if I was able to add self-publishing management (if there was such a thing) on top of the design and typesetting services that I already provided? Having learned the lesson several times throughout the life of my business of not passing up golden opportunities, I yet again 'got back in the car' and said yes.

That one phone call went on to change the face of my business forever. I not only learned that self-publishing isn't rocket science, but there is a lucrative demand from people like Paul for an all-inclusive design and publishing service. Six months later, I rebranded my business from SWATT Design to SWATT Books and have not looked back. At the last count, I have since published over 80 titles, including two of my own, and have more job satisfaction than I have ever had in my entire design career. In many cases, I am helping people achieve their life-long ambition of becoming a published author. The joy I get watching someone hold their book in their hands for the very first time is priceless. Like a phoenix from the ashes, I was able to create a new business out of the wreckage of a situation that pretty much destroyed the old one, all because I didn't give up.

"It's OK to have your eggs in one basket as long as you control what happens to that basket."

– Elon Musk; engineer, industrial designer, and technology entrepreneur

---

Lessons Learned

You could easily assume that yet another experience like this of betrayal would lead me to taking on board the lesson of refusing to trust anyone ever again, but you would be wrong. Surprisingly, even to myself, I still find it in my heart to trust people; but that trust is increasingly hard to earn.

No, the lesson I learned from TPH taking me to court was two-fold; the first very practical and the second profoundly personal.

The practical lesson is simply not to put all your eggs in one basket.

We hear this adage time and time again, but I wonder how many people truly stop to think about it. The concept behind this tried and tested saying is that if you put all your eggs in one basket and drop the basket, all your eggs could break and you would have no eggs left. The same is true in life. If you put the whole of a resource or commodity into one thing (regardless of what it is) you risk losing everything if something breaks.

In my case with TPH, I became 100% reliant on them for new business leads. Because I had so much work coming in from them, I stopped actively looking for my own new sources of work. I chose the path of least resistance because they were handing me a steady stream of vetted, ideally targeted new clients on a silver platter – all I had to do was complete the work. But it meant that when things broke, as TPH showed their true colours, I had nothing left. There were no warm leads that I was nurturing, and I was completely out of the habit of looking for new work for myself.

Thankfully for me, it wasn't particularly long or very hard to get back into the habit of actively seeking new clients as part of my daily routine. However, how much easier would the situation have been if I had never stopped in the first place? The court costs would have been easier to swallow, and things wouldn't have become quite so desperate. I might have even been able to afford more robust legal support and advice to potentially enforce the CCJ that I had been awarded.

Now think of your own life. How many vulnerable points do you have whereby if something broke you could lose everything? For example, the sole breadwinner of the household losing their job or falling ill/passing away. Being reliant on a single client for your business's success or failure. Or having all your retirement savings tied up in one investment.

Sometimes all it takes is one small event to bring about a catastrophe. Diversify. Only racehorses can win a race while blinkered.

The second, more profound, lesson is the one that seems to be a recurring theme in my life... trusting my instincts.

I saw the warning signs in some of TPH's behaviour fairly early on in our partnership, but I didn't listen to my gut. Part of me can blame it on business naivety, but not all of it. My experiences with Mr. X and the lessons I mentioned in Chapter 9 should have taught me better than to ignore the warning signs, but as it was business and not personal, for some reason the original lesson didn't feel like it applied. Guess what – the lessons we learn apply everywhere, regardless of where in life we learn them. A lesson you learn in your personal life can have just as much impact and effect on your business or professional life, because it's all *life!*

As I've mentioned before, gut instinct is there for a reason. It's an in-built reaction to danger that is meant to keep us safe and ensure the successful continuation of the species. There are instances where it's not the end of the world to ignore those fears and push forward regardless; some of the greatest discoveries and achievements of human history are credited to those who did just that.

BUT there are equally times where you ignore your instincts at your peril.

The difficulty is in knowing which gut instinct to listen to and which it is safe to ignore. I'm afraid there are no hard and fast answers to that. It's a matter of listening to your gut and then ascertaining each individual situation rationally and emotionally.

There are some people who will wonder why I say that you should look at things both rationally and emotionally – surely that is a contradiction. You hear people saying that you should weigh up decisions rationally, that emotions just cloud your judgement, but I disagree... to an extent.

When we look at something rationally, we are said to be thinking with our head; and when we look at something emotionally, we are said to be leading with our heart. Instead, I see them as being two sides of the same coin. Your head and your heart are both looking at the same problem, just from two different aspects. It would be folly to make a decision based on only a single point of view, so you should always consider both – even if you only act on one.

Use the trigger of 'gut instinct' to pause momentarily and review the situation with both your head and your heart. Then decide on whether the situation is right or if you should pull the ripcord and get out.

I have also learned valuable lessons from the success I've had as a result of the silver lining I found in the wreckage that TPH wrought. These are, that narrowing your niche is never a bad thing, and don't resist the path.

Many new entrepreneurs think that you need to cast your net as wide as possible to be successful; that anyone and everyone should be your target audience. I even see this pattern repeated by authors when they target the readership for their book.

Counterintuitively, the more you narrow your focus on who you want to work with, the more successful you will be. I really struggled with this concept in the beginning. All I could see was that if you narrowed your focus you would end up with fewer people to sell to. Fewer prospects would mean fewer sales... and who in their right mind would do that???

But that point of view is completely wrong. You just need to look at things from a slightly different angle. Yes, you are selling to fewer people; however, it means that you can target those people more accurately. You can fulfil a more specific need for those people, and if you combine this approach with adapting your language to this narrower audience, you can speak directly to them, their needs and their pain points. All of this can equate to a much higher conversion rate. So yes, you are talking to fewer people as a group, but you win a higher percentage of them. Think of the analogy of shooting fish – you'll get more fish by shooting them in a barrel then you would in an ocean.

There is also a beneficial by-product of this approach. If you get your targeting right and really nail your message, you can sell the same product or service for more than you could in a more open market. This is the holy grail of business success. Selling the same amount for more means you end up working less for the same level of return. Think of it: more time for your family, more time for enjoying life, more time for the things you value most. Because at the end of the day that is what we all want; we want to work to live not live to work.

And finally, don't resist the path. This lesson was a bit of a strange one for me, and I guess may seem a bit strange for many other business owners as well.

Many of us are taught that to create a successful business you need to have a plan and then you need to stick to that plan. But how often does life follow the plan? You need to be able to adapt and pivot that plan according to new circumstances as they arise.

As I write this, we are just coming out of 3 months of near-global lockdown due to the coronavirus pandemic. The economy has virtually ground to a halt, as nearly every business sector has been hit with being forced to close physical doors. This has created a near-universal need for businesses to pivot to a completely different way of operating to survive. Just a few months ago, no one could have predicted this seismic shock to every economy in the world, and the unprecedented effect it would have on everyone's personal and business lives. This is a stark reminder that at some point plans go out the window and you need to adapt to a new landscape. It will rarely be as dramatic as a global quarantine situation caused by Covid-19, but whatever comes along to disrupt your plan, you need to have the flexibility to go with it.

For me, in the aftermath of what happened with TPH, I could have stuck to the original plan and insisted on continuing with corporate graphic design. Despite the higher competition and the bad experiences I had had to date, with perseverance I could have made it work. But instead, I decided to see where this new path of working with authors would take me, and the gamble has paid off. I have found my niche and I am now in a far stronger position personally, financially and professionally than I was before.

Be open to new ideas and explore new avenues that present themselves – whether you are forced to or not. You never know where a new path will lead.

"You never know what's around the corner. It could be everything. Or it could be nothing. You keep putting one foot in front of the other, and then one day you look back and you've climbed a mountain."

– *Tom Hiddleston, actor (Deep Blue Sea and the Avengers franchise)*

FOURTEEN:

Concrete walls

By 2017, things had started to settle down into a somewhat comfortable routine. The rebranding and repositioning of my company into that of a full-service self-publishing consultancy was complete, I had enough work coming in to pay my bills (though not much more than that), and I felt I had finally found my niche. But something was missing.

I had no idea what that something was, just a feeling that a fundamental piece of the puzzle wasn't lining up and until I figured out what it was, I wasn't going to progress any further than where I was. I was convinced that the answer lay somewhere in the vastness of what I still didn't know about business, so I scrimped and saved until I could afford to work with a business coach. But not just any coach; I wanted to work with the best in my part of the UK and that was Ian Dickson.

I had known Ian for as long as I had been running my business. Within the first few months of starting up, I had attended a free marketing seminar hosted by Ian, and we had remained in contact ever since. I had watched as his reputation grew as a business coach, someone who helped his clients achieve astounding, tangible improvements in results, and I knew that working with him was going to be a game-changer.

Despite only being able to afford to work with Ian for a few months, I learned a massive amount from our sessions. I came away with a solid grounding in how businesses really work in terms of ensuring that everything works together in harmony like a well-oiled engine, with no one thing operating in isolation. He taught me the importance of tracking a range of key metrics throughout the business, and not just to look at the bank balance to gauge the impact of what I was doing. He showed me that nothing should be treated as purely transactional but always as a potential partnership to be cultivated.

Though I felt more in control of my business and more confident in how to manage it effectively, something still didn't feel right. The answer would come from two separate and quite different conversations.

The first was at the 2017 Business Show at the ExCel Centre in London. Ian had recommended that I visit the show to get some practice networking with other business owners (my ideal target audience) outside a structured networking meeting. I still wasn't overly comfortable talking to strangers about me or my business, and Ian saw this as a great way of pushing me out of my comfort zone.

Whilst at the show, Ian introduced me to an intimidating, larger-than-life character, Brad Burton. In front of me was a man looking the polar opposite of everything I associated with the business world – he was dressed in jeans, t-shirt and trainers, with large tattoos up both arms. He looked like a man you would pray you'd never meet in a dark alley. It turned out that despite this thuggish appearance and demeanour, Brad was the founder of the UK's largest joined-up business networking organisation, 4Networking. He was also one of the keynote speakers at the show. Brimming with curiosity to find out how this was even possible, I went along to watch Brad speak.

Brad's talk was only 30 minutes long, but I was in for the shock of my life. His brashness and northern swagger didn't disappear when he got on stage, it intensified! He unashamedly talked about his rough upbringing on the streets of Salford, getting shot at, being addicted to drugs, having no one give him a chance and, despite his past, still achieving all that he had. Regardless of the fact that every other sentence out of his mouth was laced with profanity that would make a drunken Irishmen blush, his energy, charisma and enthusiasm was infectious – I was blown away! Here was a man who had lived his life on his own terms, who literally said "F*ck it" to anyone who told him he couldn't do something and went and did it anyway. And he has gone on to achieve immense success. He has launched one of the largest networking organisations in the UK, published four books, is the highest-ranked business author on Amazon, and is a motivational speaker who major corporations and conferences jockey to book. Clearly there were more ways to achieve business success than I had previously thought.

The second conversation happened a couple months later during a routine phone call with one of my clients, Claire Brumby. I was helping Claire to publish her first book, *The Winning Mix*, and through the course of the project we had formed a close connection. Claire and I shared similar points of view on a great many things, and as the project progressed we ended up confiding in each other more and more about the things going on in our lives and businesses at the time.

I was still feeling a sense of something missing in my business, and it had started to affect my confidence. I wasn't quite in a state of depression but I could feel that I was on my way back to some of the darker recesses of my mind. Most of all, I was frustrated at not being able to pinpoint what the elusive missing piece was. The worst part was that all this emotional turmoil was starting to impact on my work; things were getting missed and my enthusiasm was starting to dry up.

I still don't know exactly how it came about, but during this routine call with Claire to discuss book marketing techniques, we got talking about how each of our businesses was REALLY doing and I ended up having a full-blown emotional breakdown on the phone. Claire listened patiently, and sympathised, explaining that she had been through a very similar experience before writing her book.

She then told me about a business support group that she was a member of called Now What Club. Claire explained how this group had supported her through some pretty tough times, and how it was more than just business owners sharing their problems; it was also a place where you could grow, adapt and work 'on' your business in a safe environment. She finished by saying that the group was run by none other than Brad Burton.

I have no doubt that Claire meant that last statement as a throwaway comment, another nugget of information with no real significance other than a bit of background. But it was the deal-clincher for me. I thought that if I could even get the tiniest bit of insight from Brad, it would be worth it. Claire put me in touch with Brad's assistant Pippa, and I joined on the spot – I didn't even bother with the free one-week trial.

When they join, every new member of Now What Club receives a one-to-one consultation call with Brad. It's a highly intense discussion, where you explain as succinctly as you can the single biggest problem you are facing. Brad then gives you direction on how to go about fixing it, with the help from other Club members. NWC members affectionately refer to this call as the "10-minute Brad-ing", as it often ends up being a brutal wake-up call. My call with Brad was no different.

The call started in typical Brad fashion: "You got two minutes kiddo, what's your biggest problem right now? GO!" I started to explain what I thought my problem was, trying to put into words this amorphous feeling of something being missing. Before my two minutes were up, Brad stopped me mid-sentence and dropped the bombshell that would change everything. "What's missing is YOU!"

Wait... what??? How could I be missing; my business WAS me???

Brad went on to explain that I was so focused on getting everything perfect and running my business in the way I believed businesses should be run that I was stifling my passion and enthusiasm for what I do. I had built a concrete wall around myself, thinking that my business was separate from me; that it was unprofessional to have anything personal cross over. The result had created a complete disconnect between who I was and what I was trying to achieve; and that disconnect was affecting everything from marketing and messaging through to how I felt about my company and my work.

He ended by saying that, as a four-time author himself, he knew that authors would not trust placing the work that they had put blood, sweat and tears into the hands of a faceless company. I needed to step up and take centre stage.

And before I knew it, the call was over. I sat in stunned silence in my office thinking, "What the hell just happened?" I had well and truly been "Bradded"!

Needless to say, I didn't get much work done the rest of that day. I started taking a cold hard look at the business that I had built and realised that Brad was right. Everything about my company, both internal and external facing, was clinical and stuffy and clearly attempting to be something that I'm not – corporate. Wrongly, I had assumed that because my primary audience was business owners that I had to portray solely a business persona to them to connect with them. I was completely missing the point that business owners are also people. They are people no different to me, and people need to build trust. Sure, people will buy purely based on brand with the likes of Apple, Amazon or Microsoft, but I'm NOT Apple, Amazon or Microsoft!

The irony is that my company name WAS my name... or at least what my maiden name had been – Samantha Watt... SWATT. I had subconsciously put myself front and centre of my business from day one, yet here I was denying my myself that role. In fact more than denying it; I was actively avoiding it.

After that, I started to re-evaluate everything I did within my company. Internally I continued to run my business according to the lessons I had learned from Ian. In order to be big, you need to think big and that meant having systems and processes in place to allow you to scale and know where you are at any given moment. But externally I tried to make my business all about forming a human connection with my audience. I started blogging and doing little videos to answer common questions. I implemented a policy that all initial consultations and design briefing meetings were to be held face-to-face with clients – even if this was remotely via video conference call. I overhauled my website to include photographs of me and added a complete bio of who I was and what my passions were. I even made the decision to finally write my first book, *Stress-Free Self-Publishing*, which Ian had been on at me for ages to write as a means of cementing ME as an expert in my field.

Though this all may seem easy and straightforward on the outside, on the inside, for me it was anything but.. I battled constantly with myself over how much of my little protective concrete wall that I had built around me as a 'person' needed to remain in place for my own safety. To nearly everyone on the outside of my life, and even to many close to me, I had learned to hide behind a façade of being normal. I really didn't want anyone to know that the real me was scared and vulnerable nearly all the time. When I had started my business, it was with a significant amount of fear surrounding the idea that Mr. X could use my business to track me down. The mere thought of him turning up on my doorstep one day fills me with dread. That was the specific reason I had found myself in the predicament that Brad had pointed out; of being too aloof and protected behind a veil of corporate secrecy. The very thing that I felt was keeping me safe was in fact holding me back. Doing what Brad had suggested meant flying completely in the face of that fear, and deep down I knew that I couldn't be half-assed about it – it would need to be all or nothing.

It has taken quite some time and a great many 'get back in the car' moments, but I have implemented all that Brad suggested I do and, suffice to say nothing has been the same since. My confidence has increased in leaps and bounds; and this time I can say that it is genuine confidence in myself, not just a feeling of belonging. I've found experiencing my position as the public face of my company oddly enjoyable and immensely rewarding... once I was able to get over my debilitating stage fright. I now enjoy my interactions with other authors and business owners, and actively seek out new opportunities where I can take centre stage and talk about the power that books can have on people and businesses alike.

I started to enjoy networking and joined Brad's 4Networking, first as a Passport member and then as a team leader – as 4Networking is a joined-up network, this means that you can 'passport' to any meeting of any group anywhere in the UK. I began volunteering to speak at 4N's unique 20-minute '4Sight' talks at numerous meetings across Hampshire and Dorset. This helped me, in small bite-sized chunks, to overcome my fear of public speaking. This led me to being able to be confident when delivering my first keynote talk when I launched *Stress-Free Self-Publishing*. I am now comfortable with the idea of being the public face of my company and owning my position as an expert.

But most importantly, I can hand on heart say that I am the happiest and most at peace that I have ever been. I no longer live in fear of what might be around the corner, because I know that whatever it might be, that I can deal with it; and if I can't I know I have a support network around me to help me deal with it.

Do I have a multi-million-pound business, a luxury yacht, a supercar in the driveway and a summer house in the Caribbean? No. Is that what defines success for me? Hell no. I have my health, I have a wonderful family, I have a business I am proud of, and I love what I do. I may still have lean months now and then, and I know I still have plenty of room to grow, improve and learn, but I have the most important things in life and that's all that really matters.

"**Always be yourself, express yourself, have faith in yourself, do not go out and look for a successful personality and duplicate it.**"

— *Bruce Lee; martial arts master, actor & philosopher*

Lesson Learned

This final lesson is one that I think every business owner needs to learn, and that is that it is OK to be yourself in business.

Far too many of us have this notion that to succeed in business you need to portray a certain persona to the outside world; that your personal life and work life are to remain separate. To a certain extent that is still true, but never to the extent that your business becomes a soulless machine.

The truth is that people buy from people, not faceless brands. Even the big corporations that I mentioned earlier have an influential leader at the helm who people can relate to. Apple had Steve Jobs, Amazon has Jeff Bezos and Microsoft has Bill Gates. The list doesn't stop there: Elon Musk (Tesla), Richard Branson (Virgin), Henry Ford (Ford Motor Company), PT Barnum (Barnum & Bailey Circus), Estée Lauder, Walt Disney and Sakichi Toyoda (Toyota), I could go on and on. All these global brands had or have a public face that you can connect with regardless of how remotely; and your business should be no different.

There is a caveat here though. The person you portray as the face of your company needs to be genuine. It needs to be the real you or else it won't work and will end up having the opposite effect. Even if you put on a good show of your public persona, if it's not real the disjunction will show through. People want to feel like they are buying from someone who understands them, who they can relate to. Understanding and relatability can't be forced; it's either there or it's not.

I know what you might be thinking: what about all the things we buy online without ever coming into contact with a single human being? It seems these days that there isn't anything that you can't buy on the internet, from clothes to cars, houses to horses. But take a moment to stop and think about your relationship with the stuff that you buy online... it's just stuff right? Regardless of its monetary value, it's just a commodity.

Now think about something that has more significant personal value to you. Regardless of its monetary value, would you buy something like that from just anywhere? No, you would want to buy it from somewhere and someone you trust, and trust can only be forged through connection. Whether it's connection with a company's owner, or through connection with other customers – there is a human element needed for that trust to be built.

Alternatively, think about something that you bought where you genuinely enjoyed the buying experience. More than likely it was because you formed a rapport with the salesperson; you felt that they understood you and your needs and cared about fulfilling those needs however they could. Again, human connection.

There is nothing wrong with injecting a level of humanity into any business, regardless of what it is. In fact, I would go so far as to say that genuine success depends on it. Humanity in business is no longer a sign of weakness or a lack of professionalism. Instead, it is a strong indicator of strength, integrity and trustworthiness, virtues that are needed in the world now more than ever – and not just in the world of business.

So, take a leap of faith and step up to put yourself at the forefront of whatever it is you do. Whether it's running a business or a campaign, selling a product or a service, raising money for a charity or fighting for something you believe in; put your true self as the driving force behind it so that people can relate to and connect with you. Let your passion, determination and drive show, and like moths to a flame your light will attract people to your cause.

"Business leaders cannot be bystanders."

— *Howard Schultz; former chairman and CEO of Starbucks*

Conclusion

So, there you have it; a peek behind the curtain of my life. This is not an exhaustive account of all that has brought me to where I am today but is at least an insight into the lessons that I have learned so far.

The challenge with any lesson is not just in the learning of it, but in the application of it throughout the rest of your life. Many of the lessons that I have recounted are still difficult to implement in practice. There are some mistakes that I continue to make, but at least now I am more conscious of them and am always striving to improve.

Interestingly, from writing this book I have realised just how much I have learned from my life and how far I have travelled. The obstacles that I have overcome to get to where I am now have made me a stronger person. I am now able to endure things that may have otherwise crushed me. I have learned compassion, conviction, patience, understanding, resilience, forgiveness and courage.

Most importantly, I've learned that the lessons never cease. I look back on past experiences and constantly uncover new lessons that lay buried in my subconscious, and new experiences present the opportunity to learn yet more. Even the experience of writing this book has taught me a powerful lesson in itself, and that is that you should never fear undertaking a difficult task just because you think it will be difficult.

When I made the decision to write *From Broken to Brave*, I was rather scared of what dredging up all these old memories would do to me. Would I start suffering from nightmares again? Would I invite back the depression that I've battled with for years? Would I start to second-guess all the decisions that I've made? Even Mum expressed concern about how writing this book would affect my mental health.

But to my surprise, not only have I not suffered from any of those issues, but I've found the entire process highly therapeutic. I've been able to come to terms with certain aspects of my past that still held some residual trauma for me. So, not only was the process of writing this book not as difficult as I had initially imagined, it has also benefitted me far more than the amount of effort this book has taken to come to fruition.

As for you, I hope you have found something of value in these pages. My intention in writing this book has always been to help others find meaning, peace and purpose in their own lives. If by sharing my story I have helped you in even the smallest way, then that work has been doubly worth it. So whatever obstacles you face in your life, know that you can not only overcome them but use them to forge a far brighter future yourself if you just have the courage to fight for it.

With love

Sam x

Lightning Source UK Ltd.
Milton Keynes UK
UKHW022106161020
371717UK00006B/13